The *Purpose* of Abundance

A 40-Day Guide to Hearing God

CHERI CHAFIN NORRIS

ILLUMIFY
MEDIA.COM

The Purpose of Abundance

Copyright © 2026 by Cheri Chafin Norris

READER DISCRETION ADVISED

This book contains references to drug use, sexual assault, and suicide.

Published by
Illumify Media Global
www.IllumifyMedia.com
"Let's bring your book to life!"

Paperback ISBN: 978-1-964251-93-6

Cover design by Debbie Lewis
Printed in the United States of America

To my friends and family. This is my Christmas gift to you.
May you hear from God. I love you so much.
Thank you for loving me too.

The Lord is my shepherd;
I shall not want.
He makes me lie in green pastures;
He leads me beside the still waters.
He restores my soul;
He leads me in the paths of righteousness
For his name's sake.

Yea, though I walk through the valley of the shadow of death,
I will fear no evil;
For You are with me;
Your rod and Your staff, they comfort me.

You prepare a table before me in the presence of my enemies;
You anoint my head with oil;
My cup runs over.
Surely goodness and mercy shall follow me
All the days of my life;
And I will dwell in the house of the Lord
Forever.

— Psalm 23 NKJV

Contents

Provision

People

Pain

Prologue

April 18, 2005

Dear God,

I hate my life. I hate myself. I hate my dad. I'm sick and tired of feeling disappointed and crying. Getting kicked off the high school morning news desk really hurt, but getting kicked off the cheerleading team makes going to school not even worth it anymore.

My graduation is coming up. I used the last bit of money I had to buy my cap and gown, and now I'm being told I may not be able to walk the stage. I passed all of my classes, but they say I have too much truancy. I'm not skipping school for no reason. I live on my own, and I have bills to pay! It costs me two hundred dollars a week to live here. I actually like it here, because I can just move out and stay in my car if I can't afford the payment at the end of the week.

There are some creepy neighbors. It scares me a little, but I keep the deadbolt locked. I get a very paranoid feeling when I get too high, so I have wrapping paper taped to the windows so people can't see inside. It's pink Disney princess wrapping paper. It helps me believe that maybe one day I will have a happily ever after.

I don't think I would struggle as badly if I was just taking care of myself. I bailed my dad out of jail last week. That was five hundred dollars. Now he's asking for another five hundred dollars to help him until he gets a job. I hope he loves me as much as I love him. I bet he'd help me if he could. I have never hated and loved someone at the same time as much as I do him.

I've been awake all night and getting ready to leave for school. I can't miss any more days. It's time for my braces to come off, but the orthodontist told me until the final eight-hundred-dollar payment is made, they won't take off the braces. I got the money though, and will take it to them today after school. I just wonder if my dad would feel bad to know I stripped on a school night to get it.

Introduction

I've been journaling for over twenty years. It's a gift and a curse. There are things I wouldn't have even remembered, had I not read about it. It's not easy to read my cries to the Lord when I felt scared and alone. I am grateful that I have so many years of writing to show me what God has done for me despite my brokenness. I already had a criminal record and a drug addiction before I turned eighteen. I know I'm not alone in that.

For the past decade, I've operated a staffing firm called Cornbread Hustle. It's a firm specially designed to help employers hire people in recovery or people with criminal records. After interviewing thousands of people who need a second chance, I learned that more people than I thought share the same experiences.

After high school, I made a commitment that I was never going to be desperate for money again. I told myself I was going to be successful and become a business owner. I did end up patenting a tanning bed, worked in a newsroom, and became vice president of a PR firm, all in my twenties. There were, however, more arrests, addictions, and bad decisions. Success was certainly not linear, and will never be because I'm human.

The biggest mistake that caused me a lot of pain was believing I was in control of my life and refusing to trust God. But how could I trust a God that let me down as a little girl? Well, thankfully I have the gift of these journals, and I can see plainly how I could trust Him and how he provided for me. These journals and my experiences have taught me that there is a cycle to obedience that leads to abundance.

As you begin to embark on this forty-day journey, I want to prepare you. You will grieve. You will grieve who you were, who you've become, and saying goodbye to the old you as you surrender to God.

This book is certainly a labor of love and I couldn't do it without God's help. I've never written more than five thousand words at once, and I'm currently approaching forty thousand words just after three days of writing. I spent seventeen hours each day writing nonstop, taking naps throughout the twenty-four-hour periods. I appreciate Him for giving me the strength to do this.

This book you're reading is God's perfect timing. Although I was not obedient to God and it took me some time, I am sure that He has you reading this book at the perfect time for your life. I wrote this book is because I want to help others feel less alone when they can't understand why they crave chaos or sabotage good things in their life. I pray that as I share my own vulnerabilities and failures throughout this book, you will be able to dissect the reasons behind these seasons of life, and be less afraid of them. I hope this book helps you explore your feelings with curiosity instead of shame.

I believe that God will put this book into the hands of the people he is trying to reach that will receive an intimate experience with Him.

Throughout this book you are going to learn how to apply the methodology I use to hear from God. I want to start off by telling you that I am a human being with a sinful nature, and I don't get this thing called life right most of the time. This book reflects that. It's a little raw and honest and confusing at times as I lay it all out there. It's also a guide, a peek into the steps God provided me to help me make better decisions. I truly believe God asked me to provide this guide to you, and I'm just being obedient with that request. The method, the cycle of obedience is *Prayer, Purpose, Patience, Provision, People,* and *Pain.*

First, I *pray.* When a thought comes to my mind, I ask God if it came from heaven or hell. Sometimes I can feel the answer right away, and other times I have to ask God to reveal the truth to me over time. If that's the case, I stay in a season of prayer until I have clarity.

Once I feel like God is telling me to move forward, I step into a season of *purpose.* This is when I act on what I feel like God is asking me to do, even if it feels uncomfortable.

The next season I step into is a season of *patience.* This is when a lot of Christians give up, missing out on a heavenly reward. Patience is hard when we are waiting on God. We start to think to ourselves, well if this was God's will, wouldn't it be easier? While God wants us to have the desires of our hearts, he doesn't want those desires to come before Him. This isn't because God has some kind of big ego and wants to see you squirm. This is because we are here to become more like Christ. If God gave us exactly what we wanted without any waiting, how would we develop character? Being in a season of patience forces us to rely on God and exercise surrender.

Next, we move into a season we all love: *provision.* This is when we get the job, we get the promotion, we get the wife, become pregnant, or anything else we have been waiting and trusting God for. In this season, we must give God the glory and share our testimony.

Then we arrive at the season of *people.* The top two commandments from God are to love Him and love others (Matthew 22:36–40). As Christians, our journey on earth is impossible without people. However, this is where the devil loves to trick us. People will disappoint us. We fear people's opinions. We take credit for our accomplishments to receive validation from people. We avoid vulnerability by not sharing our testimony of where God brought us from.

This can lead us to a season of *pain*. The devil wants us to believe that God failed us, but that's not true. We've failed ourselves. We have succumbed to our own desires that Satan tempted us with. The apostle Paul complains of the thorn in his flesh and begged God to take it from him. Paul is encouraged to take pleasure in his pain because God's grace is sufficient for his strength to be made in perfect weakness (2 Corinthians 12:7–10). It took me a while to get on board with this, but I have learned to be accepting, and even grateful for the thorns in my side. My thorns could be different from yours, as we are all uniquely made. One of my many thorns is alcoholism. This is a thorn that keeps me close to God. In order to maintain sobriety, I have to surrender and ask God for help.

In this book, I share personal stories that apply to each cycle of obedience, so you can draw from my experiences while seeking your own.

The "Prayer, Purpose, Patience, Provision, People, and Pain" cycle repeats and is ever evolving as long as we are here on earth. So, if you are struggling in one of these seasons, know that it will eventually change. As we watch the leaves fall and grow back again, we too fall and grow again. The devil wants us to hold onto shame when we fall, but that's just another nasty trick in his toolbox that he uses to keep us from moving forward with God's purpose for our lives.

If you don't have a journal, get one. I've provided journal prompts at the end of each chapter. I believe that you won't just write in this journal for the next forty days, but you will continue to stack journals for years to come as you see how God is working in your life. I strongly encourage you to take this one day at a time. Don't skip ahead. Trust the process. Be sure to set aside at least one hour each day for quiet time.

Personally, I set my alarm to wake up one hour before I need to get ready for the workday to make sure I'm prioritizing time with God. I also suggest you give up something for forty days that distracts you. For me, it's social media. Several times throughout the year, I will do a social media detox, so I can hear from God better. Social media allows the enemy to stick thoughts into my mind that begin to spiral. Specifically, I start to compare myself to others and end up feeling behind in life. Those are distractions that keep me from being aligned with God's will for my life. For you, it may be something else. Porn, trash TV, smutty books, alcohol, gaming, whatever. Ask yourself what you spend most of your free time doing, and you should be able to figure out what it is that's distracting you from hearing God.

If you have the ability to take a sabbatical with no distractions, you could spend time with God over the course of several days during a quiet retreat and work through this to get it done faster. I believe that God will work in your life whether you take three full days or one hour a day for forty days. The important thing is to be present and take the time to do the work. This won't work unless you do.

Before you get started with Day 1, write down a list of "I am" affirmations, where you want to see yourself in five years. This could be "I am an executive for a tech company" or "I am a mom" or "I am a father" or "I am happy." It could be anything you want for yourself in the near future. I don't love the word manifest, but many people would call this manifestation. I call it prayer. For me, it's basically presenting to God what I want and asking if he will give it to me.

Once you finish that writing project, you are ready to get started.

Prayer

Day 1

God Chose You

*"You did not choose me, but I chose you
and appointed you so that you might go and bear fruit—
fruit that will last—and so that whatever you ask in my
name the Father will give you."*

John 15:16

One of the most common things I hear from people when they are working to discern something is "I'm just not sure if God is telling me to do this, or if it's my own desires." If you feel this way, not only is it normal, it's by design. The devil brings confusion into our lives, and the most confusing thing he does is tempt us with our own desire.

The Bible says that God does not tempt us with evil, that it's the devil that uses our own desires to entice us (James 1:13–14). The Bible also states that the Lord will give us the desires of our hearts (Psalm 37:4). The devil loves to confuse us with seemingly contradicting Scriptures like these. Scripture goes on to say that God will align our desires with His will. This is why knowing the Word of God is so important because the devil can trick us into thinking God is giving us the desires of our hearts when it's really the enemy enticing us with our own desires.

In the garden of Eden the devil told Eve that she will be like God (Genesis 3:5). The devil tempted Eve with her own desires of having power. Even Jesus wasn't exempt from the devil's schemes. The devil tempted Jesus in the wilderness by offering him to have all the kingdoms of the world. Jesus knew Scripture, so he was able to tell the devil "Away from me, Satan! For it is written: worship the Lord God, and serve him only" (Matthew 4:10).

After Jesus told the devil to flee, the Bible tells us that angels came and attended him. How much easier life would be for us, if we were able to spot the devil's schemes as quickly as Jesus did. That's just the thing. We do have the same power Jesus had if we stay rooted in the word and in prayer and fasting with God. Scripture tells us that we have the same power that raised Christ from the dead and that God's immeasurable power is available to those who believe (Ephesians 1:19–20).

One of the many problems with the devil's tricks is when he plays a movie of our future, and it looks like it's from God. It can seem like it's good and a blessing. But the only abundance the devil is offering is an abundance of sin and pain.

One quick way I try to discern if something is from the devil or not is to ask myself if this future is promising me worldly desires such as money and power or if I'm motivated by joy and peace. Not being rooted in the Word of God is the easiest way to fall into Satan's trap. Before you know it, you're cursing God and asking Him why you're getting divorced and jobless. The devil played a fraudulent movie of your future, knowing what was really on the other end of that desire he tempted you with. That's his first party trick, and he loves to take it a step further by making you think it's Gods fault.

This has happened to most of us at some point in our lives. In fact, the devil has worked really hard to convince me not to write this book. He has presented opportunities to me to distract me from this path. I did fall for it a couple of times, but I persevered. I believe I have built a resilience to pain, which is helpful. I don't love the fact that I endured so much pain from my own self-destructive behaviors, but I am glad I have developed resilience to suffering. Why? Pain is inevitable when you are walking the Christian walk.

The apostle Peter encourages believers not to be surprised by "the fiery ordeal that has come on you to test you" (1 Peter 4:12). Once you are able to see suffering as a path to glory, you will build confidence in your discernment to align to God's will for your life. This is why God chose people like Saul and Moses and countless others in the Bible to do His work. Some of the most unlikely and unqualified people were used by God to further His kingdom. That is how God gets all the glory. If it's something that is possible with human will power and determination, there's not much room for the supernatural to work.

We are all fallen because we are human, and God loves to comfort us and pick us back up. Fear of failure has been one of the devil's greatest tactics to bring me down, and I know the best way to release shame is to shine light on the darkness and share my testimony. The apostle Paul tells us "there is no condemnation for those who are in Christ Jesus" (Romans 8:1). Shame is from the enemy; it's not from God.

God chose you for a purpose. Over the next forty days, ask Him to reveal Himself to you so you can hear what He is asking you to do.

Journal Entry Prompt

Dear God,

Today I feel like you're telling me to _____ but I need your help to discern if this is from you or my own desires. Please align my desires with your desires, so I can do what you're asking me to do with more stronger faith.

Day 2

Three Days with a Bunny

"But ask the animals, and they will teach you,
or the birds in the sky, and they will tell you; or speak
to the earth, and it will teach you, or let the fish in the sea
inform you. Which of all these does not know
that the hand of the Lord has done this?"

Job 12:7–9

God has always used nature to communicate with me. I know that's not unique to me. He loves using His own creation to reveal himself. He used a burning bush to get Moses's attention. He used a rainbow as symbol of His covenant and promise to Noah, He sent birds to Elijah, used a whale to redirect Jonah, and He used a star to reveal the Birth of Jesus.

There are many places in the Bible where nature completely changes the direction or mindset of people. Recently, I was on the back porch reading my Bible. My dog started barking at some bunnies. I felt so bad that these sweet bunnies were not only disturbed, but they were now away from their home.

One scared baby bunny made it just a few feet away and was lying down flat in the grass. I picked her up and I started caring for her. I bought goat's milk and a syringe and bottle fed her. This bunny became my everything for three days. I didn't leave my house. I didn't work. My only purpose at that time was to care for that bunny.

God revealed so much to me in those three days. I had been really struggling with trust and surrender. How could I trust a God that had let me down so much? The way I felt about that bunny and how I cared for it revealed to me how much God must love me.

There were times the bunny was afraid of me and resisting my care. It really made me look at how I do that to God. I am aware that most women get this feeling when they have a child. I think God knew I would struggle to even get there without help, so He sent me a bunny. I prayed and prayed, begging God to help me with surrendering to Him. On the third day, God nudged me to open up my journals and read about my journey.

As I read through my journals, I saw that God has been putting it on my heart to write a book for five years. He was preparing my heart, because I can say with confidence that I was not in the mental state to write a book that anyone would read. God knew I was going to have a spiritual experience with nature and that I'd be looking back at the readings when He gave me those soft whispers. In fact, that's why I'm here in this little bungalow writing these words you're reading right now.

On May 24, 2020, I had written about a vivid dream I had. There was a person unpacking a lot of suitcases that symbolized my "baggage." In the dream I was told exactly the amount of money that was going to be in my bank account soon, and to be diligent with the money.

Could this be a vision from God? I wondered. At that time I had no money, and my car was being repossessed. The dream was just so vivid, though. I wrote in my journal the amount of money I was told in my dream I would have and prayed, asking God if it was a vision from Him. In my dream I had seen the word *bungalow* flying at my face. At the time I thought bungalow meant a three-walled hut on Bali or something. I wondered if God was trying to tell me to take a trip to write a book.

Five years later, as I'm writing this book, the amount God told me would soon be in my bank account is the exact amount I have today. An amount that didn't seem possible. I was literally shaking when I realized this because I knew in my heart God was revealing Himself to me, and I was overwhelmed with gratitude and awe.

As if that wasn't a clear enough sign (God knows how stubborn I can be) that same day I received a text message from a number I didn't recognize. It was a person that worked for a church camp and retreat center in Austin, Texas. He told me that they had just finished building a building that they named the Sabbath House and told me that this is something they want to provide for pastors to get away and work on writing projects, or simply to have quiet time with God. He asked if I had any writing to do, and said God put it on his heart to invite me even though I wasn't a pastor.

My jaw dropped. He sent me a photo of the house. I googled "bungalow," and the pictures that popped up looked exactly like the house. I began to cry, and told God if he really wants me to write this book, he has to give me the words because I cannot do it on my own.

"I would love to take you up on that offer," I texted him back. "You have no idea how timely this is. When is the next available check-in."

What is something God has whispered in your heart for a long time to do, but you just didn't take action for one reason or another?

Journal Entry Prompt

Dear God,

Something you have been whispering to me is _____.
I haven't taken it very seriously because _____.

Day 3

Squirming Ants

*"Dear friends, do not be surprised at the fiery ordeal that
has come on you to test you, as though something strange
were happening to you. But rejoice inasmuch as you
participate in the sufferings of Christ, so that you may be
overjoyed when his glory is revealed."*

1 Peter 4:12–13

Until my three-day experience with the bunny, I viewed
God as a man that was holding a magnifying glass over
my body, watching me squirm like an ant burning from the
heat from the sun while laughing. "Muahhahaha! Squirm,
Cheri! All for my glory!"

You may be wondering, why I would serve a God like that.
Well, to put it simply, I didn't trust myself to do any better.
Until I got sober, I lived a very self-destructive lifestyle that
harmed myself and others. While squirming like an ant, I had
faith that whatever happened in my life would be all I could
hope for. I knew that "all things God works for the good of those
who love him, who have been called according to his purpose,"
(Romans 8:28), but I did not trust that I would have a happy
life. I thought that "all things God works together for the good
of those who love him" simply meant that God would use me
to help others, or someone would somehow benefit from my
pain. I never imagined the word *good* would be reserved for me.
My shame caused me to believe I was a bad person instead of

a person that did bad things. I didn't feel like I deserved to live happily ever after, so I would push away the gifts God tried to give me to avoid getting my hopes up and being disappointed. I struggled with addiction for fifteen years. Life seemed unfair for most my adult life, and I often felt like a victim.

When I was trying to change my habits, I was disappointed with some popular Christian self-help books. *When are they going to talk about the bad things they did before they became a Christian?* I thought. I really struggled to relate to the young mom who felt convicted when gossiping about another mom at a PTA meeting.

Maybe I was wrong, but at the time I felt like they weren't being honest about their true struggles. Back then, I thought my life was normal. I felt like everyone had been through similar things I was going through and that they must've just handled it better than I had. The irony is many of the women I speak to in prison probably see me as some polished girl who doesn't get in trouble. I'm far from perfect, but I do live a pretty stable life these days. I wake up early, go to bed early, go to church every Sunday, and I tithe. I'm consistent with going to the gym, and I read my Bible daily. This is a life I didn't know I could ever have, and quite frankly, I didn't want it. It seemed boring.

After reading a few Christian books, I decided I would write one for the "bad girls" who wanted to be good but didn't know how. That was me. I didn't know I was worthy enough to wear cute Easter dresses or be invited to brunch with church folk. I felt like I always needed to be the tough girl that was a little rough around the edges. Looking back, it was just a mask I wore to keep myself safe from feeling rejected. I didn't understand at the time that I could just simply change my mind and start behaving differently. I felt like other people had put me in a certain category and wanted me to stay there. Well, shame made me feel that way, anyways. I felt like I had a bad streak that everyone could see. That I was too broken to have a good life or be a wife to a husband that valued me for who I am and not what I do. I was afraid that anytime I did something different, like decide to get sober or dress differently, people would remind me of who I used to be. And they did. In fact, it still happens. The difference between then and now is that I don't take it personally now.

I've healed now and worked through my stuff enough to know that those who want to keep me in a box are projecting their own insecurities. Sometimes your failures make others feel better about themselves, and your success can do the opposite. Sometimes they are simply protecting themselves from disappointment—especially if you've hurt them with your addictions. My point is, often when someone reminds you of who you were, they are not doing it to harm you. They are just doing it. Understand that it's all part of changing your life. If it were easy and felt good, everyone would do it. It took time for you to build your old reputation, and it will take time to build a new reputation.

If you are in a season of transformation, keep going. God is going to bring new people into your life who pour into you as you become the person that will attract those people. If I could go back in time, I would spend less time convincing others who I was becoming and why I was doing it. That was just me trying to convince others, so I could eventually convince myself, because I didn't fully believe it was possible for me. My worth was still in what the world thought of me, not what God thought of me.

Many people I have worked with are church hurt. They were hurt by the church and have formed an opinion about Christians. I understand. I formed an opinion about men and vowed to never trust another man again or get married. Yet I went back to men and bars over and over even though they caused me pain. I never blamed the place, but instead I blamed God for not being there for me. How many times did you go back to a person or place that hurt you?

I found so many reasons to justify not going to church, starting with calling what I thought were the Christian hypocrites. I wasn't wrong in thinking that way, and neither are you. Even Jesus called the Pharisees hypocrites. You can read the red letters for yourself in Matthew 23:13. If you are new to reading the Bible, the red letters are words that Jesus actually spoke. I tried to only focus on reading the red letters when I began having a relationship with God, because the other stuff gave me too many questions. At the time, I wasn't ready to explore deep theology topics.

You may have been hurt by religious people, but how many non-religious people have hurt you? Here's the thing, we are all broken. People in the bar, people in the church, people in our own households. This is where the cycle of prayer, purpose, patience, provision, people, and pain come into play. We can't avoid being let down, but we can lean on God for help and understanding.

I would quit going to church when I saw one thing happen that I didn't like, yet I would be in places that had several bad things going on because it was good for my business or ego. God has changed my mindset. I won't stay in places that don't align with what God wants for me, but I will continue to go to church.

At first when I went to church, I felt just like a number. That worked for me because I wanted to come late, leave early, and blend in. If that's how you feel, that's okay. God knows your heart and will be patient with you. Talk to him and let him know how you feel. Now, I am part of a congregation that notices if I am not there and will text me if I miss service. I have an amazing relationship with the pastor and can call or text him anytime for prayer or guidance. At some point I wanted to do life with people and not just be a number. It takes persistence, but it's important. God is not glorified when we turn our backs on something that is supposed to make us better.

I know this can be really hard for some of you to read and even potentially make you feel angry. It's okay. Be angry. Cry. Scream. Tell God how you feel about church and Him. God wants your passion and your emotions. He wants a relationship with you. Just like you become passionate enough to fight with a spouse, God expects us to be passionate enough to fight with him. Tell him how you're hurting. He can handle it, because he already knows. Ask him for help.

Journal Entry Prompt

Dear God,

The way I viewed you is _____. This has affected my relationship with you. Please reveal your true nature to me by _____.

Day 4

Shallow Waters

*"See to it that no one takes you captive
through hollow and deceptive philosophy, which depends
on human tradition and the elemental spiritual forces
of this world rather than on Christ."*

Colossians 2:8

What comes to mind when you think of a shallow person? It's easy to view a person with shallow traits as someone who cares only about external validation and who tends to focus on superficial aspects of life. Notice I say a person with shallow traits instead of labeling a person as shallow. I do not like labels, because what we do isn't who we are. We are God's children who are learning how to live in a broken world.

A person with shallow behaviors can lack depth, intellect, or emotional understanding. People don't sign up to be shallow, just like people don't sign up to become addicted to drugs. It just happens. Life happens. I had shallow traits before I found Jesus. I'm a deeper person now, but I still have to be cognizant of slipping back into my shallow ways that were developed over the years. Some examples of shallow behavior include not being able to have a deep conversation, changing the subject when it's about meaningful topics, not being concerned with how other people are doing, being obsessed by how they are perceived by others, having an excessive focus on superficial things like appearance and material possessions, not able to understand or connect with others' perspectives, having little to no genuine connections, and thriving on gossip and drama. I really hated to type this out because I saw myself in all of it. I have had to rewire and retrain my brain to want a life of peace over chaos.

Being aware of your character defects gives you power over them. It has allowed me to invite Jesus in to help me. We aren't born shallow. That's not how God made us. We become hardened by the world and painful experiences we've endured. Perhaps feeling abandoned by people you love or being betrayed by someone you trusted trained you to keep things superficial and people at arm's length. Maybe the devil took a hold of your insecurities to keep you in bondage. The great news is God is the author and the finisher of our faith (Hebrews 12:2), and he has already defeated Satan (Colossians 2:15).

My parents loved me very much, but they became hardened by this world. They were in love and married for twenty years, but they didn't display their affection. I saw them kiss on the lips one time, and it gave me a giddy feeling as a child. I loved love, I just didn't know how to give it or receive it.

My parents come from a generation that is all about picking yourself up by the bootstraps and keeping your problems private. Therapy wasn't an option. My parents' idea of therapy was threatening to send me to bootcamp every time I stepped out of line. Many parents from that generation parented that way. I was raised to "do as I say, not as I do."

My parents couldn't give me what they never had. My dad's mom dropped out of school in the third grade to help on the farm, and his dad suffered with alcoholism. My mom's mom also drank a lot, and her father traveled often. My mom resented having to take care of both of her sisters when her mom was on a bender. My parents had their own pain and struggles, but I always knew they loved me.

There are two incidents when I saw their true love for me, and their vulnerability. The first incident was when we were on our last family vacation in Florida before my parents divorced. My brother and I were old enough to go by ourselves to the beach shops, so we were out on a walk. I asked my brother if he wanted to race across the street. I took off running without looking. As I reached the median something knocked me on my back and knocked the wind out of me. Just then, a giant truck went flying by in front of me. My brother and I were so shaken up we turned around and went back to our beach house. When we walked in, my dad was sitting on the edge of the bed with his head in his hands sobbing and praying. He was speaking in a language we couldn't understand. (Now I know that he was praying in tongues.) I asked him why he was crying. He said that he had a horrible vision that I had been hit by a truck, and God put it on his heart to pray for me. How do you even explain that? From that incident alone, you would think I would know both of my heavenly Father's and my earthly father's love for me.

The second time I witnessed my parents deep love for me was at a Chilli cookoff as a family. I was about eight years old. I climbed way high in a tree, pretending to be a cat. I said to the people below "I'm a cat! I'm an expert tree climber." Famous last words. The branch broke and I fell many feet down to the ground. The next thing I remember was riding in the back of a tractor in my mom's lap. My head was bleeding, and she was holding my head in her lap. I was in and out of consciousness, but I saw her crying. She even said, "It's going to be alright baby" and leaned down and kissed my forehead. I felt so much love at that moment.

Maybe that's why I put myself in so many dangerous situations and acted out as a young child. Perhaps I wanted to experience those moments of love again from my parents. Chaos and drama are where I usually felt loved by others. Otherwise, I felt forgotten. I am not at all blaming my parents for my behavior, I am just working to understand why I misbehaved as I did. Emotional safety and vulnerability are gifts. If they are not given to us, they are hard to give. For me, I have learned that Jesus is the ultimate gift of emotional safety and vulnerability.

Journal Entry Prompt

Dear God,

Emotional safety and vulnerability for me looked like _____.
If I have become hardened by this world and developed shallow traits, please reveal it to me and heal me so I can love and be loved better.

Day 5

Childlike Wonder

"Like newborn babies, crave pure spiritual milk,
so that by it you may grow up in your salvation."

1 Peter 2:2

Life hasn't always been so difficult for me. I had a great childhood. My parents were married for twenty years, and they had good, stable jobs. They always provided for me. I never wanted for anything. In fact, my brother and I were pretty spoiled. I was in pageants. I had private softball lessons. I went through a modeling school where I learned about dinner etiquette and how to sit up straight and walk with good posture. I was privileged.

I loved Power Rangers, and, of course, the pink Power Ranger was my favorite. I was such a prankster. I had fart machines, fake bugs, fake poop, and anything else I could prank people with. I definitely got that from my dad. I loved to have sleep overs with my girlfriends, and we would dance the night away to TLC and Spice Girls. Baby Spice was my favorite. I loved to put my hair in pigtails and dance around the house in platform shoes. My dad wasn't very happy about the outfits, though. He was always very protective of his little girl and never liked it when I dressed like the girls on TV.

I also had a very nurturing spirit. I had baby dolls that I would pretend were real, and I would care for them by pushing them in strollers, feeding them with fake milk, and putting them to bed in their crib. I put hearts around boys' faces in the yearbook and would plan my future wedding. I did all the things little girls do. I always believed in a happily ever after, that is, before the disappointments.

One of the exercises I have people do in prison workshops is to write down all the things they loved to do as a kid. Many of the people I serve have become so broken, they forgot what it's like to experience joy, which I understand all too well. Take a moment right now to write down all the things you loved to do as a kid. You will be surprised how God was shaping you.

God gave me the gift of storytelling. I used to love to hold a fake microphone and talk into my dad's video camera. I would always say, "Hi, I'm Cheri, live in the flash!" It was so cute, because I couldn't say my *Rs*. I'm smiling as I write this, because I now realize I was just repeating what my dad used to say which was actually "live in the flesh." Either he had it wrong too, or he just never corrected me. As an adult, I ended up working in a newsroom.

In second grade, I would buy balls of yarn from Walmart and braid bookmarks together. I would go door to door and sell them for two dollars each. One time, a man said "Wow, you want me to buy a two-dollar bookmark when the whole ball of yarn costs less?" He chuckled and still supported me, but that was my first lesson in entrepreneurship. I remember going back home and reevaluating what my retail price would be. Later in life, I patented the first-ever tanning bed you can inflate, deflate, and take with you. I also loved to play teacher when I was little. I remember the only thing I wanted for Christmas was an old-school overhead projector, the kind teachers used from the sixties to the nineties. God gave me a passion for teaching. What I didn't know is that I'd be teaching inside prisons, but that's just how God is. He helps us turn our pain into purpose.

If I could go back in time, I would tell the little girl version of me that drugs and alcohol feel really good, instead of telling her to "just say no." If you were in grade school between 1983 and 2009, you most likely participated in the Drug Abuse Resistance Education Program. I believe it would've been more helpful for me to hear the truth: "You may like the way you feel after you drink alcohol and do drugs, but the problem is you'll most likely believe you'll never have as much fun as you once had before you tried it." It didn't help that I would see adults be in a great mood and look happier when they drank alcohol. We just didn't know what we didn't know, and many of us fell into addiction, and wondered what happened to our lives. There is no shame of where you've ended up. We did the best with what we knew at the time. As we begin to know better, we do better.

My personal sober journey included doing a lot of things to make me feel like a kid again. I joined a roller derby team because I love to skate. My number was 828 as a reminder that God works all things together for good (Romans 8:28). I also tried my hand at painting. I'm a terrible painter, but it was very therapeutic to paint while I talked with God, because I was very anxious in my first couple of years of sobriety. I would go to the movie theater and watch cartoons and go to amusement parks. I basically relived my childhood with God's help.

Remember what it was like to believe in Santa Claus? When I think about the childlike joy and wonder I had as a child, asking Santa for stuff I wanted, I think of my relationship with Jesus today. The Bible clearly states that God values childlike qualities: faith, humility, trust, innocence, and dependence on Him. Jesus encourages believers to become like children to enter the kingdom (Matthew 18 2–4). The more I step into joy and let go of my doubts, the more I feel like a kid again. What can you do over the next few weeks to feel like a kid again?

Journal Prompt

Dear God,

As a kid, you showed me _____. I always loved to _____ but life hurt me by _____.

Day 6

Ignoring Jesus

"So, as the Holy Spirit says: 'Today, if you hear his voice, do not harden your hearts as you did in the rebellion, during the time of testing in the wilderness.'"

Hebrews 3:7–8

It is hard to live with conviction. It is hard to choose the right thing to do when the world says it's okay to do the wrong thing. The Holy Spirit will convict us when we are doing something that isn't pleasing to God. Conviction is not the same as shame, although many people confuse the two—including me. Conviction is when the Holy Spirit makes someone aware of their sin and gives them a desire to turn away from it. The devil loves to confuse us, making us believe that conviction is condemnation.

The Bible tells us that "there is now no condemnation for those who are in Christ Jesus" (Romans 8:1). The devil tries to get us to believe that God is shaming us, so we will want to ignore Jesus. Think about it. If you were shamed by a therapist, would you go back? No! When your friend is shaming you, do you want to spend time with them? Of course not.

If we allow the devil to let us believe that Jesus is shaming us, we will find comfort elsewhere. Unfortunately, anywhere we try to find relief from our pain other than in the arms of the living God is a trap the devil sets for God's children. That's when the shame spirals out of control. The places we go for comfort (drugs, sex, work, pornography) brings more shame, which leads to seeking more comfort, which leads to more shame. This spirals into a deep pit of despair we can't get out of.

On Christmas Eve 2018, I was driving to my mom's house about an hour and a half away from me. Typically, it was an easy drive. I would drink some alcohol and listen to music, but I couldn't that year because I had to keep a breathalyzer in my car for a year as one of the conditions of my latest DWI. I'm not sure why I liked to drink and drive instead of just drinking at home. I assume it was the same reason why I would pace when talking on the phone. I always needed to be in motion or else my body was set on fire with feelings.

With two months sober, I was hearing God's quiet whispers. He was really putting it on my heart not to drink. Looking back, I know he was giving me a way out and giving me strength to resist temptation. I just didn't want to receive the peace he was offering, so that Christmas it was a long, anxious drive. I had never greeted my family without at least a little bit of alcohol running through my blood stream. The dysfunction in my family was very hard for me to handle emotionally. It was easier for me to drown my resentment than accept responsibility for my own life.

There is zero healing with that approach. It gives everyone but you power over your feelings. If the way others behave affects how you feel, you are not allowing Jesus to be in control of your life. That's why we need to surrender daily. People are always going to disappoint us, so we need Jesus to comfort us.

On the way I stopped at the liquor store to get some vodka. Something (God) kept telling me to get a case of sparkling water. The last five minutes of the drive to my mom's house, I had so much anticipation for that handle of vodka in my passenger seat. It was sitting on top of the case of sparkling water and next to a bottle of blue Gatorade. That was my thing before I went just about anywhere. I would park, open my car door, pour out three-quarters of the Gatorade, and replace it with vodka, the more odorless booze.

After two months of not drinking, I could feel that first drink go down my throat and coat my belly. The feeling of the alcohol blanketing my insides was one of my favorite feelings. Alcohol was my security blankie. Today, I'm blanketed with the peace of the Holy Spirit, but back then, I was accepting what the enemy had to offer.

I walked into my mom's house peppy and smiley because, like a fussy toddler, I finally had my blankie in hand. It was a typical family Christmas. Lots of drinking and a gift exchange. I was successfully drinking the sparkling water I bought in between every alcoholic drink I had to keep me "sober." I believed that if I didn't black out, I did not get too drunk.

During the gift exchange, I received this really neat lava lamp with jellyfish in it. By the end of the night, most of my family were drunk. I was practically drinking my Topo Chico with my pinky up because I felt so much pride that I was the least drunk. *I did it,* I thought. It was the first time for as long as I could remember that I controlled myself. It was about three in the morning, and I was sitting alone on the bar stool, relishing in my success that I had beat alcoholism. As the jelly fish went up and down in the lamp, I had a thought. *If I name the jelly fish, and remember their names when I wake up, I am not an alcoholic.* So that's what I did. I named them Kirby and Oscar and went to bed.

The next morning came in just a few short hours. I lay there with my eyes open. I didn't have a headache, but I was more anxious than I had been when I wasn't drinking. I thought, *You have got to be kidding me. All of this time I've been drinking to solve my anxiety, but is it actually causing it!* I shuffled into the kitchen to make coffee. I wasn't surprised that I was the first one awake. I've always been an early bird, even when I was drinking. I lifted myself up on the bar stool, looked at the jelly fish in the lamp, and said, "Kirby, Oscar, I think I'm done drinking."

Journal Prompt

Dear God,

Lately you have been convicting my heart of _____. I haven't listened because I've found counterfeit comfort in _____.

Day 7

You Can Run, but You Can't Hide

"Seek the LORD while he may be found;
call on him while he is near."

Isaiah 55:6

What better Christmas gift to give myself than the gift of sobriety? It seemed like a good idea until New Year's Eve rolled around a week later. I always thought New Year's Eve was for amateurs, and I rarely participated in drinking. I liked to start the New Year off with good intentions at least. But since I had been sober for a week and didn't know when I would drink again, Near Year's Eve was very difficult for me. I tried to stay busy until the sun went down so I could make it another day sober, but social media was triggering me. I was feeling lonely. Typically, I would go to a movie to get past happy hour and come outside to darkness and go straight to bed. There wasn't a movie I wanted to see that night, so racking my brain on what I could do that would keep me safe from drinking alcohol, the idea of going to church came to my mind.

Wow! That would be boring, I thought. But I knew there would be music and no alcohol. I found a church that was holding a New Year's Eve service. When I pulled into the parking lot, I could not believe how many cars were there. *Do this many people not have anything else better to do on New Year's Eve?* It was a big church packed with people worshiping on one of the biggest party nights of the year.

As people held their hands up in the air, I couldn't help but to think these people were desperate to believe in something to feel better about their life. It's not that I wasn't a believer, I just didn't have a relationship with God, so I didn't understand worship. It felt like the music went on forever. I can say that I used to go to church selfishly just to hear a message that would motivate me. I had no concept of what it meant to sing praises. Now, it's my favorite part of the service, because I know what it is to feel God.

And that's just what happened that night. Everyone was singing, "Come alive dry bones." I felt that same warm blanket feeling, only this time it wasn't alcohol coating my stomach. It was the Holy Spirit. I didn't know that at the time, but tears started rolling down my cheeks and warmth and comfort came over me. I remember saying to myself, *I have dry bones. I need to come alive.*

When the pastor came out, he gave a great sermon about second chances. I was very encouraged by that, because I was struggling to keep my second chance staffing agency profitable, because I needed a second chance myself. That night I felt the omnipresent (everywhere all the time), omniscient (all knowing), and omnipotent (all powerful) God. Right before the service was over, the pastor said he wanted to do something crazy. He wanted to hold a worship service every night for the next six nights to kick off the New Year the right way: with God. It sounded excessive but maybe that was what I needed to help me get six more nights of sobriety. So I went to church every night for the first week of 2019, and I achieved another week of not drinking.

A couple of weeks later, I was in my bathroom curling my hair when I realized the last couple of weeks had been easier in terms of my sobriety. I thought that maybe God was helping me, but I didn't pay much attention to it. I felt an urge to look at my Bible. It wasn't an audible voice or anything, just a feeling. I learned what the phrase "God put it on my heart" meant in that moment. I felt it.

On that day, I felt God speak to me through my heart. I ignored the first nudge. My Bible was downstairs, and I was trying to get ready for the day. The nudge became so strong that I had to get my Bible. I am glad that I was obedient to that nudge because it changed my life. I told God that if he was trying to get my attention to make it clear, to have me open the Bible to a Scripture that applied to my problem. I flipped through the pages of the Bible, and with my eyes closed I pointed my finger to a random page. When I opened my eyes and saw the verse, I threw the Bible at the wall and fell down on the ground crying.

"Help me then! Give me help if you want me to stop! Make me not want it! Take this away from me!" I yelled and then sobbed and sobbed, cursing at God. Later, after growing in my relationship with God, I learned He actually wanted this from me. God doesn't mind my complaints; He already knows them. He wants me to talk to him about them. And boy, did I! After reading that verse that day: "wine is a mocker and beer a brawler; whoever is led astray by them is not wise" (Proverbs 20:1), I knew I was on a new walk, and it was with God. I knew I could run from God, but I could not hide.

Journal Prompt

Dear God,

I have been running, but I know I can't hide from you. Today you are telling me that I need to _____.

Purpose

Day 8

Finding Purpose

"In him we were also chosen, having been predestined according to the plan of him who works out everything in conformity with the purpose of his will."

Ephesians 1:11

M any people want to know their purpose in life. That's why the famous inspirational book *The Purpose Driven Life* has sold over 50 million copies. For most of my life I believed I was just simply a creative person who could create stuff from pain. While God certainly gave me the gift of creativity, he also gave me my purpose before I was even born. The Bible says that even the very hairs of your head are all numbered (Luke 12:7 and Matthew 10:30).

My resistance to God allowed the devil to make the journey harder for me. As I sit and read over twenty years of journal entries, I can say with confidence that "every good and perfect gift is from above, coming down from the Father of the heavenly lights, who does not change like shifting shadows" (James 1:17). Typically, our sinful behavior causes our unhappiness. Sure, things happen that are out of your control. You know, those things that make you ask, "Why, God, why?" I think all of us at some point have asked the question "If God is all knowing and all powerful, why would he let terrible things happen to good people?"

One thing that has taken me a long time to comprehend is that we live in a fallen world. The Bible says that all good things come from God. It doesn't say God is going to keep bad things from happening. In fact, the Bible is clear that suffering is inevitable (John 16:33), and our ultimate purpose is to love God and love people. How would we change and grow if everything were easy and there was no pain? It takes pain to change. The apostle Peter encourages believers to rejoice in suffering (1 Peter 4:12).

When I was sixteen years old, I was in jail for the second time for theft. My first arrest was when I was fifteen, but my parents bailed me out, chalking it up to peer pressure. The second time I had to actually do a little time for the crime. I had to spend a couple of weeks in jail and wrote letters every day to my parents. I'm glad I have these letters to see what my mindset really was at the time because all I can remember is the shame, pain, and embarrassment from the thought of my cheerleading team gossiping about me that I was in jail over the holidays. That's how the devil works. He takes your circumstances and works hard to get you to believe that God abandoned you and isn't good, and that *no good things* come from God.

In these jailhouse letters, I wrote about being very grateful about the fact that for the first time in my life I felt like God was actually sitting next to me. I didn't know it at the time, but God was giving me a spirit of joy, even in the worst of places. My letters were bursting with gratitude. In one letter, I told my parents I couldn't wait to come home and do laundry for everyone, because I had learned what's it was like to do laundry for strangers, without pay. I had even wrote that I was grateful for the fact that I was getting used to the nasty food, and it started to taste good. Looking back, I am in awe that I was grateful to be eating Thanksgiving dinner in jail.

What blew me away the most, though, is that at the young age of sixteen, I wrote that I believed that God gave me a purpose to change my life and come back into jail and give people hope and help them see their potential. I can't get over how blessed I am to have these letters. It is a blessing to see God's hand on my life and to see that I was on fire for the Lord in that jail pod.

It surprised me to read that the other inmates were mad at me for reading Scripture to them and sharing with them that God had a purpose for their lives. I do not remember any of that. All I could remember is that my parents abandoned me, God abandoned me, and I was not worthy of a good life. The devil did exactly what he set out to do. He made me feel unworthy and believe that God did not have a purpose for me. In fact, three years later I journaled that "God is no longer sitting next to me. The devil is. But God is behind me sitting next to Jesus saying that I'm not deserving." That obviously wasn't true, but that's what the devil had me believe. I can see it clearly in these letters that it has always been my purpose to help people in prison. I just struggled to get better because I didn't realize that it was God's help I needed, not my own.

When I got out of jail, I forgot all the great things God had told me and done for me while I was alone in my cell. The rejection and shame of the real world came tumbling down on me like a ton of bricks. My parents sold my car while I was in jail because I lost my driving privileges, but that wasn't the worst thing. My boyfriend of two years broke up with me. He was a godly man that didn't want to deal with my toxicity anymore.

That jail stay should've been what changed my life. It says so in the letters. I had vowed to start going to church and have a relationship with God. All it took was some consequences from my own actions to blame God for my misfortune and continue living for my own selfish will. Things got a whole lot worse before they got better.

You may not have letters to look back on like I do, but were there moments in your life that God was there for you, but you forgot what he did for you because of disappointments and rejection? Can you think of examples where you got glimpses of what your life could have been but ignored it because the devil convinced you that God didn't think you were worthy enough?

Journal Prompt

Dear God,

I have always felt like a part of my purpose of loving you, and loving others is that you gave me the gift to _____. I haven't been using it because I have felt _____. Please give me the strength and guidance to get into alignment with your will for my life.

Day 9

Hustlin' Cornbread

"Many are the plans in a person's heart,
but it is the Lord's purpose that prevails.'

Proverbs 19:21

For the next fifteen years after high school things continued to get harder for me. After being released from jail, I ended up becoming dependent on drugs and alcohol and wondered my way through life while trying to gain approval from the world. I was so embarrassed by my past, that I wanted to take back everything I lost and prove to everyone that I was enough. The irony of that is I didn't believe it myself.

After barely graduating high school and getting clean from meth, I decided to get back to my roots and do what I loved. Before the drugs, I had pitched to my principal that I wanted to create a news station to anchor the news to the school every Friday. I convinced him to allow me to do a casting call for a weather person and sports anchor. I loved writing scripts, reading the teleprompter, and seeing myself on TV in the classrooms on Friday mornings. I felt so accomplished.

It was a short run though, because only a month after beginning my career as a high school news anchor, I tried meth. It only took a few weeks for the school to decide I was no longer a fit. Of course, the school didn't know I was on meth, but they couldn't deal with my tardiness and poor attitude. They also couldn't understand why I was having a hard time reading the teleprompter without slurring my words or going cross-eyed. It was because of the lack of sleep. I would be up for days at a time and didn't realize how badly it was affecting my appearance and performance.

After getting kicked off the news desk, I felt bitter watching someone else anchor the news, which wouldn't exist had I not created the station. Looking back, I realize they had no choice. I needed to be pulled off the news desk. I had also gotten kicked off the cheerleading team, and quit the softball team. This all happened in just a matter of months during my senior year.

A couple of years after high school, I decided I would get a job in a real newsroom. Many people told me it would be impossible because I did not have a college degree nor the drive to go to school. I often felt confused about my path in life, but one thing was for sure, college just wasn't for me.

People were not wrong. I applied for news jobs for years and never got any call backs or interviews. One time I received a letter in the mail from a news station. I was shaking I was so excited to open it. It was a rejection letter. At least they let me know, but honestly being ghosted felt better than being told I didn't make the cut.

While I was trying to get a job in the newsroom, I got a job as a gymnastics coach. I was on a quest to experience the things I lost when I got on drugs my senior year. To this day, it's still one of my biggest regrets. Anytime there is an alumni event for my high school, I show up. It helps me relive what I lost, and I'm grateful my cheer coach allows me back as an alumni despite the fact that I was kicked off the team. Looking back, I believe many of the teachers and coaches knew I was having a hard time. They just didn't know how hard or what was really going on.

It was 2009, and I had spent a couple years coaching gymnastics while applying to news jobs. I finally got to a point where I didn't care if I looked stupid or not because I already felt so stupid for applying to news jobs for years without any callbacks. I decided to do something creative. I called Pizza Hut and asked them if I emailed them my resume, would they print it out and tape it face down on a pizza box, and then deliver the pizza to the hiring manager at CBS. I asked them to write on the back of my resume: "If you hire me, I will deliver." It worked! I couldn't believe it. I got an interview, and I got the job. I was on cloud nine.

That CBS badge that allowed me to get into the newsroom felt like my ticket to move on from my past. I felt like I had made it. Now everyone from high school would see that I wasn't worthless after all. The problem was I had a God-shaped hole I was trying to fill with achievements. I continued to fill that hole with anything the world said was successful. I had just turned twenty-three and already was working in the fifth largest market at CBS and owned a patent on a product selling on TV. None of that was enough though. I still felt worthless.

As usual, God brought me back to jail to show me what my purpose was. This time, I went in as a volunteer. Someone had suggested that I volunteer for the Prison Entrepreneurship Program. The first event ignited my passion and drive to help people in prison see their potential. The problem was, I was pouring my life into other people while filling myself up with alcohol. I had thought that since I was clean from meth and I was successful- getting drunk was just part of the whole "work hard, play hard" thing.

God still used me to help people, even though I didn't know how to help myself. I would sit down with people in their halfway houses and help them find and get jobs. I would cold call businesses and pitch people as great employees and vouch for them.

Benny, the first person I ever helped, told me he learned how to draw and paint in prison. His artwork was amazing, and he had told me that he wanted to paint murals for a living. I said, "Well, let's google a mural painting company in Dallas and pitch them!" Benny had never used Google before, because he had been in prison the last twenty years. It was a joy watching him learn this technology for the first time. The first mural company I called ended up offering Benny a job. Seeing his selfies in front of his work, which was a mural for a kid's church hallway, made my heart swell. I felt like I helped him change his life and become successful.

That was my problem. I was taking the credit for helping people change their life, instead of acknowledging that God was working through me. During my first years of helping people find employment God was working "for the good of those who love him, who have been called according to his purpose" (Romans 8:28) not because of me but despite me. I thought it was because I was smart, but it was God working through me despite my inability to be sober. Today, Benny earns six figures and loves his career.

Do you have a gift that God gave you that you feel like you are squandering? Looking back, I see many opportunities I had that I did not steward well. I experienced a lot of pain that I could've avoided had I just done things God's way and not my way. What does "doing it God's way" even mean? I'm still trying to figure that out, but I know it starts with meditating on Scripture each morning and asking God for wisdom to stay in alignment with his will. It means leaning on God to give you direction for what to do next. Everything we need to be fulfilled is found in the Bible. You can have success as defined by the word on your own, but joy, fulfillment, and true peace can only come from God.

Journal Prompt

Dear God,

The area in my life where I could lean on you more to give me direction is _____. A habit that is holding me back that I am afraid to let go of is _____. I know it's causing me to not hear from you the way you want me to hear. Help me, God. Please.

Day 10

Rock Bottoms

"But you are a chosen people, a royal priesthood,
a holy nation, God's special possession, that you may
declare the praises of him who called you out of darkness
into his wonderful light."

1 Peter 2:9

Before I got sober, I had to hit more than one rock bottom to wake up. Rock bottom probably isn't the best way to describe it. It's more like getting to a point of needing Jesus. My "rock bottoms" these days look a lot different. Rock bottom for me used to be jail and relapses, but now it looks more like difficulty in my relationships, struggles leading, or anxiety. We will get into what surrender looks like later in this book.

My last arrest was a couple of years into owning Cornbread Hustle. Yeah, the CEO of a staffing agency for second chances gets arrested for a DWI in the middle of the day. Not a good look. I went from being one of the most successful people I knew my age to living out of my car and being on probation. I felt trapped. I was going through an IRS audit that lasted a year, I had a negative bank account, and I had a terrible credit score. Once again, I was back to where I was when I first got clean from meth. Except this time, I wasn't starting from nothing. I had a business and was responsible for employees. It was truly the hardest time in my life.

From the age of fifteen, I had numbed my feelings with drugs and alcohol. For the first time in my life, I had to face my feelings head-on. I became very suicidal and struggled to fight the voices telling me to kill myself every single day. Image and success had become so important to me, and here I was homeless, broke, and jobless. After everything I had overcome since high school, I was back to where I started: living out of my car. This happened because I relied on myself and took credit for all of my success; I was doing it my way. I wanted to straddle the fence and have the blessings from God while living like I wanted.

Many people who help others avoid helping themselves. It's a very normal thing to want to focus on other people's problems to avoid looking at our own. This is why America loves reality TV so much or why embarrassing moments for others go viral on social media. Because of my own experiences, I will never post anything negative about anyone on social media or even engage in any posts that tear people down. Looking back at letters from middle school and high school, I see how other people's words chipped away at me one comment at a time. I did not have a relationship with God the way I do now, so I was not equipped to handle rejection. Now, I know God has a plan for everyone, and I do not want to be an instrument of the devil to make someone believe they aren't worthy.

How you make people feel is so much more important than what you have. How you make people feel can change the trajectory of someone's life for the better or for the worse. Words are powerful. "The tongue has the power of life and death" (Proverbs 18:21).

Do you have any patterns in your life where you find yourself wanting to give advice you don't want to take for yourself? Do you have a motive to help others that is coming from a wrong place? Are you helping others because you want to impress God? Or are you helping people because you want to impress people? No judgement. I fell into this trap myself, and many do. God already knows your heart. Be honest with Him and ask Him for forgiveness and for help to help yourself before you try to help others.

Journal Prompt

Dear God,

One of the ways that I am trying to pour from an empty cup is _____. Please reveal to me how I can allow you to refill my cup before I try to pour into others.

Day 11

Trusting God in Business

"Many are the plans in a person's heart,
but it is the Lord's purpose that prevails."

Proverbs 19:21

Psalm 23 is one of the most famous chapters in the Bible. It's one of my favorites because it shows God's provision, protection, and guidance. If there is any chapter to memorize, it's that one. It begins like this: "The Lord is my Shepherd; I shall not want" (23:1 nkjv). Let's break that down. It says the Lord is my Shepherd. A shepherd is someone who cares for sheep, protecting, guiding, nurturing them.

Then the psalm continues: "I shall not want." This means that God is enough and whatever we need, He will provide. Looking back at all my journal entries, there was never a time I didn't have what I needed. He always made a way.

This is my favorite part of the psalm: "He *makes* me lie down in green pastures" (23:2 nkjv). You see that? It says He makes me. It doesn't say He encourages or suggests we lie down; He *makes* us. This is why I try to be obedient when God is telling me to do something, because I know He is going to make me anyway, one way or another. To endure less pain, I would like to do it His way instead of trying to do it my way, because I do indeed want greener pastures. Who doesn't?

I was one year sober when Covid hit. *How am I going to stay in business when the news is saying businesses have to shut down?* I thought. I had worked so hard to maintain sobriety and keep my company afloat despite being audited and living out of my car, couch surfing. I felt like this would be the nail in the coffin for Cornbread Hustle. It was already hard enough to get companies to pay me to hire people with criminal records. Now companies wouldn't be hiring because they would be shut down.

Looking back at my letters to God, I had been very upset and felt like He had put me through hell just to stay sober. I started to despair. *I may as well drink if my life is going to suck anyways!* I thought. *At least that way I wouldn't feel it as bad.* But I knew in my heart that drinking would only make things worse, so I stayed sober, reluctantly and with bitterness toward God. Now, I think it was so healthy that I was angry with God and talked to him about it. There were so many times in my life that I only wanted to talk to God when I felt good about myself. I'm so glad I've learned that God doesn't work that way. He is a best friend. He wants to hear your grievances; He wants to comfort you.

One morning right before Covid hit full swing and our nation shut down, God woke me up at three in the morning. I was wide awake and felt the urge to get up and spend time with Him. God had given me a clear vision that I needed to buy hazmat suits and disinfectant, so we could position ourselves to be essential enough to keep our jobs. Since I was only one year sober, with no money, I had to go into debt to make this happen. I had no fear, though, because I knew this was from God and I was going to do whatever it took to make it happen. So I did.

We quickly pivoted from a staffing company to a disinfecting company. Our phones were ringing off the hook, and I was able not only to keep my employees working, but I was able to hire more people, including one guy who had hit his own rock bottom. He was facing ten years in prison for assaulting a public servant during a DWI arrest. I hired him to disinfect churches on the weekend for ten dollars an hour. A Christian health sharing company called WeShare sponsored us to do this work for pastors at no cost. During the few months that he worked for us, he ended up watching enough sermons that the weekend before he went to prison, he got baptized.

He was sentenced to ten years but got out in five years, and we were there as he walked out those prison doors to greet him. I was blown away by what God revealed to him when he was in prison, and how God comforted him. He went in knowing very little about God and came out knowing Scripture like he's been reading the Bible his entire life. That's just another example of God working all things for the good of those who are called according to his purpose. Sure, this person probably didn't want to sit in prison for five years, but look what God did with it.

People say all the time that God will take away whatever you put in front of him. That can sound scary and mean, but I see it as love. God allows you to go through things that will bring you closer to Him, which will give you heaven on earth and eternal life. I can't think of a greater example of love.

There were so many times I felt abandoned by God when He was just allowing me to seek Him to draw me near. What a gift that we can miss out on realizing if we allow the devil to convince us otherwise. I believe that my employee getting baptized before going to prison was the best thing that happened during Covid, but something else happened. We earned one hundred thousand dollars in revenue the first month we announced our disinfecting services. As you read in the previous pages, I have worked hard my whole life to be successful and come up with money generating ideas. This was my first ever one hundred thousand dollars I had ever made as an entrepreneur, and I made it in a month! I couldn't believe it!

Reading my journal entries to God during that time made my eyes water because I was like a little girl running to her daddy saying. "Look, Dad! Look, Dad! Look what happened!" I'm sure God was smiling back thinking "Yes, Daughter. I know. I had this planned for you, and My plans are always good." And good they were.

We disinfected warehouses, which were considered essential businesses. One day I was cleaning a toilet when a human resources manager asked me where I find my employees. I shrugged and said, "Prison. Where do you find yours?" He told me their workers weren't showing up to work because they were making more money sitting at home on unemployment. He asked me how I get my workers to show up. I remember it like it was yesterday. I stood up slowly from cleaning the toilet in my hazmat suit. I took off my gas mask, looked at the manager, and said, "Well, they aren't eligible for unemployment because they have no work history." God did it. He made my business vital. Because I was obedient and listened to what he told me to do, I now had businesses reaching out left and right wanting to hire people who were just released from prison.

The following year we made $5 million in placement fees because we were able to prove that people with criminal records are great workers and deserve a chance.

Have you let God get in the driver seat of your decisions? Or are you driving and only taking direction from Him when it's convenient or comfortable? God isn't going to give you something to do that won't work. Will it be hard? Yes. Will the devil attack you and make you want to give up? Yes! But no matter what, God will work all things out. It may not look the way you want it to look, but He'll do it if you submit to Him. I can promise you I never wrote in my journal that I wanted to have a multi-million-dollar company helping people coming out of prison by way of cleaning toilets. At the time, I complained about the Covid setback and having to clean toilets, but looking back, I am so grateful that he allowed me to be humbled and learn what it looks like to lean on Him to run my business and know that his ideas are better than mine.

Journal Prompt

Dear God,

I haven't allowed you to make the decisions in every area in my life. One area that I have held onto tightly and kept you out is _____. It's not working the way I want it to work, and I need you to take over the driving. Please help me have the courage, strength, and faith to walk the path you set out for me.

Day 12

Your Gifts Aren't Yours

"I always thank my God for you because of his grace given you in Christ Jesus. For in him you have been enriched in every way—with all kinds of speech and with all knowledge—God thus confirming our testimony about Christ among you."

1 Corinthians 1:4–6

The apostle Peter reminds us that our gifts are not for personal gain, but for other believers and for the glory of God and building up the church (1 Peter 4:10). It's easy for me to forget this if I'm not diligent with staying in the Word and leaning on God and not my own understanding (Proverbs 3:5). The Bible reminds us that we are the hands and feet within the body of Christ (1 Corinthians 12:12). Diverse members of the church, like hands, feet, eyes, and ears, are all part of the body and all are important and interdependent. This is why we should not be jealous of someone else's gifts. Their gift is no better than yours, it's just different.

God made your gift different, so we would have to work together to glorify Him. The problem is, we often work against each other and not together. You've probably heard that opposites attract. The reason opposites attract is because God designed it that way, not to annoy us, but so we can complement each other. He puts people in our lives whose gifts are opposite of ours, so we can work together and have the help we need.

We mess this one up in marriage. We turn to divorce when we can't work out our differences, when it was God's design that we help one another with humility and love instead of hate and shame. Over the past twenty years, I did not want to share my gifts with some of my family members because I didn't want to be manipulated. I would keep a mental scoreboard. If I did something for someone, I expected them to do something for me. I didn't even want anyone to celebrate my birthday or help me with anything, because in my mind, I would owe them. I did a really great job at keeping people at a distance and only being in casual relationships with no commitment. I thought I was protecting myself, but I was only digging myself a deeper hole that I would need God's help to pull me out of.

This put a strain on my life. I now know that unconditional love is freely given. Like the love Jesus has for us. While people can't love unconditionally the way God loves us because of our emotions, scars, and fears that stand in the way, I was told that when you have a child of your own, that's the closest you'll get to understanding how much God loves you. I can't wait.

God has softened my heart over the years, and my resentments have slipped away. As I have been more gentle with myself and forgave myself for my past, it makes it easier for me to forgive others and share my gifts freely without fear of being used. When I am following God, nobody is able to use me, because He will make all things right for me. If I'm doing what God is asking me to do, it's not up to me how the other person receives it. It's up to Him to bless me however he sees fit, and it's my job to pray for others. When we die and go to heaven, God isn't going to remind us of the bad things we did. He's going to ask us why we didn't use the gifts he gave us to serve others.

Journal Prompt

Dear God,

One of the gifts you gave me that I'm using to only serve myself is _____. Please help me use my gift of _____ to serve others. I will start now by doing _____.

Day 13

Hustlin' Junk

*"Whatever you do, work at it with all your heart,
as working for the Lord, not for human masters, since you
know that you will receive an inheritance from the Lord
as a reward. It is the Lord Christ you are serving."*

Colossians 3:23–24

It takes a lot of practice to be obedient when God asks you to do something. I recognize how hard it is. God has been telling me for six years to write a book to glorify Him and help others learn how to hear Him. Honestly, I was afraid to write a book about my faith. *What will people who used to buy drugs from me think? What about my family, who has seen me at my worst? Will people think I'm a fake or a fraud?* To put it simply, I had imposter syndrome, and I allowed the devil to wreak havoc with that.

My biggest fear is that people will think I should never make another mistake again because I wrote a devotional. I am a flawed person, and I still have a lot of stuff to work through. I don't do anything illegal, and I love God and people to the best of my ability, but I am still human. I have to hold my thoughts captive and give them to Jesus on a daily basis, or I can start to slip. I still gossip when I get angry at someone, I cuss when I'm in a foul mood, and I am not always grateful for what I have. The difference these days, though, is that I feel the conviction from the Holy Spirit when I do these things, and I ask God for forgiveness and for strength to do a better job next time.

When I first turned my life over to God, I had a really hard time enjoying life because I felt like I needed to be perfect, and if I wasn't, I felt like I was letting God down. That couldn't be further from the truth. God already knows my flaws and that I'm going to let Him down. There are no surprises for God when we do anything we should or shouldn't do. We are the ones surprised by God. God doesn't need us. We need Him.

The past couple of years I have practiced listening to God and being obedient with the gifts He gave me. One day, God gave me a vision for a junk hauling company. I remember saying out loud, "You're crazy, God. No!" But it was one of those instances when God kept hitting me with this nagging voice, making me feel like I needed to move forward with urgency. I told God I needed a sign, like a big sign to move forward. The last thing I wanted to do was run a trash company. I already did the whole janitor thing; I didn't want to do the trash thing. *Have I not been humbled enough?* I thought.

The next morning, I opened my front door to get the mail, and I kid you not, there was a giant dumpster right across the street with the words "RENT ME" painted on it in big letters. I just shook my head and shut my door, standing there in disbelief. Hoping it was just my imagination, I slowly opened my door again. Yep, it was still there. You'd think that was enough of a sign for me to move forward, but it wasn't. I was being taunted by signs (literally, signs) everywhere. I finally told God, "Okay if you want to do this, you'll have to make it work. This one is all the way on you, because I don't want to do this at all." I ordered three books about junk hauling and invested $120,000 into equipment. As I stepped through rat poop–filled abandoned houses and went to stinky junk yards, I knew it was God's plan because we were getting work and people were getting jobs. We were able to hire a homeless veteran who went on to get housing and became one year sober. God will certainly use your gifts to serve others if you let Him. Letting Him is the hard part, though. The rest is easy because God does the heavy lifting as you trust Him.

Journal Prompt

Dear God,

Lately you have put it on my heart to _____, but it makes no sense and I'm afraid. Can you please give me some signs over the next few weeks that this is something you want me to do?

Patience

Day 14

Avoiding Danger

*"Trust in the Lord with all your heart and lean not
on your own understanding; in all your ways submit
to him, and he will make your paths straight."*

Proverbs 3:5–6

You may be like me and think the idea of being led "by still
waters" (Psalm 23:2) is boring. I would rather go white water
rafting on class V rapids. I have come to a place in my life where I
have learned firsthand that God's still waters aren't boring.

Looking back at my journals, it appears that I always went
after the forbidden rapids. There were plenty of times when I
knew so and so wasn't the right man for me, but I wanted to fix
him; or I knew God didn't want me to do drugs, but I did them
anyway. There were even places where God did not want me to
go, but I went anyway.

I don't understand why I was so rebellious at such a young
age. I had a good childhood; I had everything I needed. Yes,
I had already learned to cut myself and make myself throw
up after eating in the sixth grade. I didn't even know why I
was doing it. I was just doing it. I tried my first hit of acid in
the eighth grade. Truth be told, it really scared me. I was at a
place I shouldn't have been. The high school boys thought it
would be hilarious to give me a tab of acid to see how I acted.
I remember riding my bike home and thinking I would get hit
by a car because the roads were all wiggly. When I got home

in my bed, I thought I was swimming in a pool because I had a blue futon bed. It was a terrible feeling, and I was upset those boys did that to me. I do not know why I got such a rush going places I shouldn't have gone to.

Journal entry after journal entry included letters between my friends and me talking about what kind of trouble we could get into. I also chose boys who didn't choose me back. There was one boy in particular who I wrote about often. He was cheating on me and treating me badly. He ended up getting arrested and receiving a life sentence. I don't know why I was so hung up on him.

When I was about fifteen years old, I worked at a pizza place, and this older guy (maybe in his late twenties) I'll call Jose came in and told me he owned a modeling agency. He said I was pretty. He was a regular, and would always tell me he saw so much potential in me. One day he told me to sit in his lap. I was too scared not to do it because I didn't want to lose my shot at being a model.

One night, he invited me to a party. I told my dad I was going to ride with a girlfriend to a party, and he said it was okay as long as I was home at a decent hour. The only thing he asked for was the address I was going to, just in case. When I got to the party, I definitely knew I was way too young to be there. These weren't just teenagers. They were grown adults in their twenties and thirties doing drugs. I was swimming in the pool and overheard someone telling Jose that he needs to stop bringing young girls to his house and to make me leave. Jose told me to get out of the pool because it was time for me to leave. As I got my towel, he handed me a Coca-Cola. I told him I didn't like Coke. He got furious and told me models don't turn down drinks. I apologized and drank it. Then Jose took me inside. The next thing I knew, I felt paralyzed and couldn't move. Jose threw me against the wall was trying to rip my bathing suit off. I opened my mouth to scream, but the words wouldn't come out.

Miraculously, my dad, my hero, started banging on the door right on time. I heard someone yelling from the kitchen, "That young girl's dad is here. I told you not to bring her!" Jose threw me on the ground and spit in my face and walked off. I slowly got to my feet and stumbled to the front door and got into my dad's truck. He didn't say anything on the ride home, and I was so dizzy I was about to puke. To this day I wonder why I didn't get in trouble for being so impaired. I also wondered how my dad had the intuition to come get me. I wonder if my parents had just thought it was my first time to get drunk and decided to just let it go. I never told them what happened because I didn't want them to not let me go to anymore parties. Also, I didn't want my parents to find out I was at a party with adult men.

There were so many times I needed my parents help, but I was afraid to tell them what I had gotten myself into, so I just dealt with the consequences of shame in private. This is why it's so important to teach your children how to hear from God. You don't want them to hear from the world and not know what God is saying. If we don't hear from God, the devil has no problem using other people to lie to you. It's not so hard for me to know what's not for me now that I've been sober for six years and hear God clearly.

When I first got sober, I really struggled being with this guy I knew wasn't right for me, but I didn't want to be lonely. Most of all, I didn't want to open my heart up to someone only to have it crushed. I was afraid if that happened, I would relapse over heart break. I was trying to be in control by choosing relationships I could predict. If I knew they weren't good for me, then I wouldn't care if things didn't work out. It was just what I expected. That's how self-sabotage works. It's easier to settle for something you know won't work out instead of working for something good only to have the rug ripped out from underneath you. That's why so many of my employees do something to lose their job or quit right after they receive a promotion. They struggle to handle something good, and start to feel out of control. I rarely self-sabotaged anything professionally because being successful was my mask.

One day I was walking my dog at a nice park. I dropped her leash, and it spooked her. She ran from the leash with it dragging behind her. She ran into the street and all the way back to a place she felt comfortable: home. However, by doing that, she gave up the beautiful park and put herself in danger. *Okay, God, I see what you just showed me there*, I thought.

What are some people, places and things that aren't for you that you continue to keep in your life because of familiarity? You know what they are. Are you willing to let go of those things and trust that God has something better in store?

Journal Prompt

Dear God,

I know I should not have _____ in my life and you want to remove it from me, but I don't want to let go of it. I am going to let go, because holding on hurts too badly. Please comfort me while I navigate this change and please give me strength.

Day 15

Illusion of Control

*"No one can serve two masters. Either you will hate
the one and love the other, or you will be devoted
to the one and despise the other. You cannot
serve both God and money."*

Matthew 6:24

There are so many areas in my life I've worked so hard to
control. They all were just illusions of control, though.
When you think you can control something, really it's controlling you. The year before I quit drinking, I worked so hard
to figure out how I could drink while still being able to blow
into my breathalyzer and drive my car. I spent hours planning
and preparing for how I was going to still fit drinking in my
life. I was determined to control my drinking. Obviously, it was
controlling me.

Another illusion of control I had was thinking I was Miss
Independent. I was never going to let another guy hurt me
again. After all I had been through, I justified using men for
money and flirting to get what I needed without caring about
how I made them feel. I was a certified man-hater. I thought I
was in control, but in reality, they were in control of me. We
were simply using each other and justifying it.

Eventually one of us, if not both of us, would get hurt. There
are so many stories of men who assaulted me or broke my
heart, but I forgive them. They were broken just like me, and

hurt people hurt people. If I want to be forgiven for hurting people, then I need to forgive those who hurt me. That doesn't mean I need to ever have those people in my life again, but I can certainly pray for them, and I do. It takes two people to maintain a transactional relationship. Someone has to give, and someone has to take until one person decides not to anymore. There are many people who live life with transactional relationships. All of my relationships used to be transactional until I learned the love of Jesus. Now, I strive to make sure all of my relationships are relational.

Sure, there will always be give and take, but there isn't a score board anymore, and my time spent with people is authentic without any motives besides building a relationship. I'm not perfect at this, and I still have to check my motives on a regular basis, because I learned how to have transactional relationships at a very young age for survival. God has helped me unlearn those behaviors and trust him though. The more I trust God and learn that he will take care of me, the more I can comfortably build relational relationships which require vulnerability.

That brings me to my latest illusion of control that took a lot of prayer and therapy to get through. At around three years sober, I was able to finally face hard feelings around relationships and begin to believe that there was a future for me with a good guy. I decided to write letters to my future husband. Every single month I would write a "Dear future husband" letter and just tell him about my month and my fears about meeting him and opening my heart up to him. I didn't believe anyone would receive these letters. It was just for me to start getting comfortable with the idea of being vulnerable without having to actually be vulnerable with someone.

A couple of years later, I was in Colorado visiting my mom's cousin, and she had asked me about my dating life. "God will bring me the right guy when he's ready," I responded.

"Well God isn't going to just bring someone to your door-step. You need to take some kind of action," she replied.

I brushed her off. A couple of weeks later, she asked me how it's going with finding a man. I laughed and told her nothing has changed. No man on my doorstep yet. She nudged me to download a dating app and told me to put myself out there. I cringed at the idea. I was more ready than ever, though, because at that point I actually had hobbies outside of getting drunk and didn't dread the "what do you like to do for fun" question. Since I had worked to learn how to be a kid again through sobriety, I had plenty of stuff I liked to do for fun.

I downloaded a Christian dating app called Upward and figured I could at least meet someone who loved Jesus like me, and we could go from there. I'm not going to lie, I was afraid dating another Christian would be super boring. I was still addicted to a rush when it came to relationships, which is why I thought I was better off single to protect myself from . . . myself. I knew the type of men I picked. I didn't trust myself.

After I downloaded the app, I picked some pictures and uploaded them with a couple of sentences about myself. I was about to leave for a meeting, so I only had time to match with one guy. I wasn't even sure if I was attracted to him, but his bio said he was in prison ministry, so I figured at least we could talk about *that* instead of *us*. I matched with him and forgot about it for the rest of the day.

As I was driving to one of my meetings, I saw a giant bill-board that said UPWARD all in capital letters. It had nothing to do with the app, but it reminded me to check. Sure enough I had a message from the guy I matched with. He asked what my dogs' names were. Because I had seen that billboard, I engaged in conversation.

We messaged every day for over a month. The day we were finally supposed to meet, he didn't send me a text. He had texted me a "good morning" text every day up until that day. I was so disappointed. I thought to myself, *I knew it! He's married!* I cried my eyes out telling God it was mean joke and asking why he'd let that happen to me.

I got a text later in the day from the guy and he said he was so sorry that his text that morning was undelivered and that he too was disappointed when I didn't write back. It was just a simple technical issue that had us both in a meltdown. We decided to meet at a Costco of all places. He had joked that he's a catch because he had a Costco membership, so I challenged him to take me there for our first date. That was two years ago.

I struggled so bad to just let him be a man and take the lead. I kept trying to be in control by insisting I pay for dates (even though he wouldn't let me) or making plans before he could even surprise me with any. I did this because it gave me an illusion of control. He couldn't disappoint me if I could set it up. I would insist on planning a date and paying for it, so I could tell my friends he sucks because he doesn't plan any dates. I literally set him (and me) up for failure, so I didn't have to risk being disappointed or being vulnerable. I didn't know how to ask for my needs. I didn't know how to receive his love. I didn't know what was the matter with him that he wanted someone like me. I had so many problems it felt like I was in my first year of sobriety all over again. I felt so many feelings at once that I didn't know what to do with them.

Feeling feelings made me not want to be in the relationship, but I also didn't want to break up with him. I was in a very miserable spot for a while because I didn't know how to let this guy love me, and I was making everything hard because of my illusion of control. In reality I wasn't controlling anything besides my efforts to sabotage a great relationship that God was trying to give me. That guy did end up proposing to me. His name is Ben. I wish I could say things got easier after I decided to marry him, but they did not. I got even more scared and started to spiral with fear.

One day a mentor told me: "Cheri, why do you need to know before the end of business each day if this guy is the one for you or not? Why can't you just enjoy a good relationship and trust that God will reveal to you when the time is right if he's the one for you. Trust God that he won't let you walk down that aisle confused or scared." As logical as this sounded, I just couldn't calm down my nervous system.

Things did get better and better though. Ben was very patient and understood that my bad days were not a reflection of him. They were a reflection of my own emotions that I was struggling to process. I would literally fight with air. I didn't know how to be in a stable relationship. It felt boring and predictable. It was so hard being with someone who loved me when I felt like I had nothing to offer. Most of the time I was pushing him away because I didn't feel like I deserved him.

What illusion of control are you holding onto in your life?

Journal Prompt

Dear God,

I have felt so in control of _____ but it's controlling me. Please help me learn how to trust you so I can stop trying to control this area of my life.

Day 16

How to Surrender

"Be still, and know that I am God; I will be exalted among the nations, will be exalted in the earth."

Psalm 46:10

When first cultivating my relationship with God, I would read every book I could trying to figure out how to surrender. I wanted to let go of control, but I didn't know how. I didn't trust what life would do to me if I didn't try to control everything. I had endured so much already I didn't want to risk more pain.

The devil did a number on me. Most of the good things I have in my life today were delayed because of my own fears. The good news is, if it's God's plan, it won't be stopped. What He wills comes to pass. He wanted me to write a book, and I eventually wrote a book, after a five-year delay. He wanted you to read this book, and you are reading this book.

It took me five years to write this book because I still didn't know how to surrender, and the only way I was able to finish it is because God worked through me. I surrendered my will and desires to God, acknowledging His authority and sovereignty. Now, I'm able to sacrifice my personal desires when I know God has something better for me because I've learned what that looks like. For me it meant dropping everything, turning on my out-of-office email responder, and driving out of town to get it done. I knew being obedient to God and allowing him to use my gifts to bless others would bring me more peace and joy than any of my own plans could.

Surrender looks different for everyone. We all have different desires, and we all hold onto control in different ways. For some people, surrender could mean letting go of a job that became their identity. For others surrender could be deciding to do life without drugs and/or alcohol. That was my first big surrender, and it was really hard, but not as hard as surrendering to vulnerability. At least I knew giving up alcohol was good for me and would keep me out of trouble. For my sobriety, I keep my mental health in check by doing things like journaling, going to therapy, taking hot baths, working out, going for walks, eating junk food, basically all the things we do to decompress without using drugs or alcohol.

Being in a healthy relationship was another thing. It triggered me. It threw my nervous system out of whack. I was confused because I thought relationships were supposed to make you feel good. The problem was that the relationships that made me feel good were bad for me. It's like healthy food. You have to acquire a taste for it. That was my problem. I didn't want my new life yet, but I knew I couldn't have my old life either. I was in that in between where I was trying to become who Christ called me to be, and I was having growing pains. I never had a problem breaking up with or ghosting someone I didn't feel like talking to anymore, so I knew this guy was different and it drove me crazy. I would beg God to just tell me if this guy was the one for me or not.

God wanted me to put my faith in Him and to surrender to Him, so he wasn't going to give me the answer. Reading back through all my journals, I had no idea if Ben was the one. I was too afraid to break up with him, yet I was too afraid to marry him. I needed clarity. I have learned that this is actually a very normal feeling for women with a lot of trauma. I needed wise counsel, not from people would say, "Well if you're not hot and heavy for him, he's not the one." A trauma-informed therapist helped me understand that I wanted to push this good guy away because I was afraid I would lose him anyway.

In the midst of this turmoil, I made one of the hardest decisions I had made. I surrendered my pride and got on anxiety and anti-depressant medication. For five years God had brought people into my life who told me that medication would help me. As someone who took so much pride in personal transformation and positive change, I did not want to surrender to medication. I did not want to lose control over my brain. I felt like my brain was the only thing that helped me survive because of my creativity and ability to make money. I no longer wanted to suffer though, and I was tired of fighting.

The day I took that first pill I cried and cried. I grieved what I thought was the loss of control. Turns out surrendering that control helped me trust God at a whole new level. I am able to enjoy my relationship with Ben, and now I crave peace and predictability. Everything in life I once was scared of, I'm in love with. I just didn't know how to allow myself to enjoy the gifts God was giving me because I had been through so much.

Medication may not be your answer. In fact, this book is the first time that I have ever publicly admitted to taking medication. I didn't want anyone to know because I felt embarrassed. Now I feel proud that I did something so scary to become a better person. I was one of those people that thought trusting God with your mental health meant praying away the anxiety. Yes, do that. But just like buying glasses to see better doesn't make you any less of a Christian, neither does taking medication. I took a leap of faith and trusted God with my mental health. Whatever is holding you back from trusting God, I hope you learn to let it go and put your faith in Him.

Journal Prompt

Dear God,

One thing I have said I'll never do is _____. But what I just read is confirming that I should take another look and explore that as an option. Can you help me decide if this is something you want for me? If it is, will you help me take a leap of faith?

Day 17

Naming Abundance

"For since the creation of the world God's invisible qualities—his eternal power and divine nature—have been clearly seen, being understood from what has been made, so that people are without excuse."

Romans 1:20

Abundance looks so different for me today than it did even a year ago. Over the past year I went down a rabbit hole to find out what abundance looked like for me. Literally. As I told you on Day 2, I spent three days with a bunny, and it made me realize what God's love was like for me. God used a bunny to help me learn how to love.

After spending three days with the bunny, I decided it was time to set it free. I wanted to keep that bunny in my bathroom, so I could make sure nothing bad would happen to her. But I knew she did not want to live in my bathroom. Wanting the best for her, I went out and bought about two hundred dollars' worth of supplies to make a bunny mansion for her. I put it outside and put the bunny in her new house. I thought she could have freedom but still live in my backyard. About an hour later, I went outside to check on her and she was gone. Even though I had built that beautiful house for her and gave her all the food she could want, she left. It was another reminder for me how I turned away from all the good stuff God was giving me and how it must've made Him feel.

I had named the bunny Abundance because during those three days I recognized what abundance really looks like. It's not money or possessions. It's about love. Abundance is just God and nobody else but God, but all the gifts God gives me is icing on the cake. I realize that I'm in my own little bunny mansion in this world, and God keeps building it bigger with people and purpose for my enjoyment *and His*. I know now that God wants me to enjoy my life and be happy. Like the bunny, I was just afraid of what he had to offer and ran away from it.

Although I was sad that Abundance had left, I felt grateful that God sent me one of his creatures to teach me what it looks like to feel abundance and hope for the future. For the first time ever, I felt like I was ready to be a mom. I really needed to feel that before I could be excited about it. My fears were standing in the way of any excitement I could have. I had truly believed that God brought me an early Easter gift by sending me that bunny at the end of March. I also realized the significance of three days.

In the Bible, the number three signifies divine wholeness, completeness, and a time of significant divine intervention or fulfillment. The most prominent example is Jesus' resurrection on the third day. If that's all that happened, that would have been enough, and God helped me have a whole new perspective after those three days.

It didn't end there, though. I'm overjoyed to share that the bunny did come back. On Good Friday of all days. Thank you, God.

Journal Prompt

Dear God,

I thought abundance looks like _____, but I'm starting to believe it looks like something much different. I think it looks like _____. Please send me a sign or make a way for divine intervention so I can experience abundance Your way.

Day 18

Where Your Treasures Are

"Sell your possessions and give to the poor.
Provide purses for yourselves that will not wear out,
a treasure in heaven that will never fail, where no thief
comes near and no moth destroys."

Luke 12:33

Yesterday we saw what real abundance looks like. Today we are going to talk about your treasures. Jesus said "where your treasure is, there your heart will be also" (Matthew 6:21). This verse emphasizes the connection between a person's priorities and their affections. It suggests that whatever a person values will ultimately capture their heart and attention. This is a good time to talk about what or who you are serving.

A lot of people don't like to admit they are following anyone. You know, born to be a leader not a follower. It's so funny to me. I grew up hearing that phrase from my parents, but we are in fact born to be followers. If you aren't serving God, you're serving someone or something. The Bible says we cannot serve two masters "for either you will hate the one and love the other, or you will be devoted to the one and despise the other. You cannot serve both God and money" (Matthew 6:24). This is where people really start to become uncomfortable. I was one of them. I wanted to follow God, but I didn't want him involved with my money. The idea of tithing made my skin crawl. I didn't want to give my money to the church.

One way to get real about what or who you are serving is to look at how you spend your money and time. How much time or money do you spend glorifying or worshiping God? I'm not asking you this to make you feel ashamed, I'm simply asking you to take inventory of how you spend most of your time and money so you can see who or what you are serving.

In my first year of sobriety, I read that we should not "store up for yourselves treasures on earth, where moths and vermin destroy, and where thieves break in and steal. But store up for yourselves treasures in heaven, where moths and vermin do not destroy and where thieves do not break in and steal" (Matthew 6:19–20). Man did I hate this verse. I remember calling a spiritual mentor and complaining that I don't want to wait until I die to have my treasures. "I want them now!" I cried and said it was unfair of God to expect me to live a miserable life and wait until I got into heaven to enjoy the fruits of my faith. I couldn't have been more wrong in my thinking.

In the Lord's prayer, there is a line that says, "your kingdom come, your will be done, on earth as it is in heaven" (Matthew 6:10). Today, I can confidently say that my treasure is where my heart is, which is with God, and I *do* get to experience the fruit of my faithfulness because with God, I get to experience heaven on earth by hearing him.

Most of my journal entries start with "Dear God," but a good many also start out by saying, "Beloved Cheri." These were letters that God was writing to me. He was directing my steps and telling me what was to come. The best way for me to hear from God is through writing, with a pen and paper.

There were times I was wealthy by the world's standards, but poor in spirit and there were times that I was poor by the world's standards, but wealthy in spirit. I will take spiritual wealth any day over financial wealth, because I know the best is always yet to come if I just believe in God. No matter what situation I am in, with God, it feels so light. Jesus says that His yoke is easy and His burden is light (Matthew 11:30). Allowing God to tell me what to do every single day has made all of my burdens so light.

One of the burdens that wasn't so light was the burden to surrender to Him control over my money. Money felt like my only security. There is only one place in the Bible where it tells us to test God. The Lord is chastising the Israelites through the prophet Malachi. He says: " 'Bring the whole tithe into the storehouse, that there may be food in my house. Test me in this', says the Lord Almighty, 'and see if I will not throw open the floodgates of heaven and pour out so much blessing that there will not be room enough to store it' " (Malachi 3:10). Well, that sounds convincing, but it takes a lot of faith to believe it.

If giving ten percent of your income to God makes you uncomfortable, I get it. I have good news for you, though. I've tested it for you. I got so tired of being in charge of my company and struggling to make ends meet that I told God if He wants the company to succeed, then it's His problem. I made it His responsibility by giving Him the burden. I thought if it's true that God wants to be glorified, then He has to make this work. I had to be okay with the fact that Cornbread Hustle may not be in my future, and a blessing from Him could mean being redirected to something different that would serve him better. This was very scary for me, because my company had become part of my identity.

Paul teaches us that "our old self was crucified with" Jesus (Romans 6:6) and to "put off your old self, which is being corrupted by its deceitful desires" (Ephesians 4:22). These phrases refer to the idea of prioritizing God's will and desires over one's own desires and self-centeredness. It doesn't mean the literal death of one's physical self, but rather a death to the old self dominated by sin and turning to a new life in Christ.

You know that Scripture where Paul says: "For me to live in Christ, and to die is gain . . . for I am torn between the two. I desire to depart and be with Christ, which is better by far" (Philippians 1:21, 23). Paul was not suicidal, and he didn't want to literally die. He was just suggesting a close, personal relationship with Jesus that he would experience fully after death. He even said that living in the body will mean fruitful labor, indicating the value of his ministry to others. I can relate to Paul, as living here on earth is not easy.

Fighting my own desires to die to self is not easy in a world that promotes doing whatever you want to be happy and then posting it on their highlight reel so others will envy you. Remember, real treasures are from heaven. All the beauty, possessions, and money in the world can't fill the God-sized hole in our hearts. Someone can appear to have it all on the outside, but on the inside, they have nothing to show for it. Kind of like a piggy bank with a couple of pennies in it. Shake it up, it'll make a lot of noise, but it's empty and has nothing on the inside to show for all the noise. A full piggy bank makes a lot less noise.

I was once that piggy bank that made a lot of noise and had little to show for it. On the outside, I was living large. I was hosting parties for a variety of companies, attending Dallas Mavericks and Dallas Cowboys games with great seats. I had a high-rise apartment with a nice view, and I had a fancy Cadillac CTS-V I couldn't afford. I've been on social media for twenty years. It's easy to go back and look at the old me and compare her to the new me. I'm always tempted to delete old posts, but one woman who had come out of prison told me she looks at my old posts to see what's possible. She told me that my old posts remind her of where she's at now and the new me shows her where she can be one day.

I don't want anyone to ever believe they can't do what I've done because of the bad things they've done or where they come from. With God, anything is possible. We are not to "conform to the pattern of this world, but to be transformed by the renewing of your mind" (Romans 12:2). God is renewing my mind, and my desires are different than they used to be. I went from living beyond my means in order to present an image of success to the world to living beneath my means with no debt, because I care more about what God thinks of me. If I want it but can't afford it, God doesn't think I should have it yet, and I'm okay with that because His plans are better.

Journal Prompt

Dear God,

I spend most of my time and money on _____. I would like to try to serve you better, but I need help increasing my faith. Can you help me have the courage to align my treasures and heart with your will for my life?

Day 19

Pride Prevents Provision

*"When pride comes, then comes disgrace,
but with humility comes wisdom."*

Proverbs 11:2

When I began my sober journey, someone that was helping me told me that one of my character defects was pride. I got angry and told her that I didn't need to work with her anymore since she didn't know what she was talking about. It makes me laugh to think about it now. If you don't think you struggle with pride, you're wrong. We all do. In fact, one of the signs of a prideful person is someone saying that they are not prideful.

The apostle Paul wrote a letter to Timothy in which he outlined some fruits of a prideful heart. People who are prideful are

> conceited and understand nothing. They have an unhealthy interest in controversies and quarrels about words that result in envy, strife, malicious talk, evil suspicions and constant friction between people of corrupt mind, who have been robbed of the truth and who think that godliness is a means to financial gain. (1 Timothy 6:4–5)

When I read through the list, I am reminded of just how easy it is to fall into prideful behavior. We read that "Pride goes before destruction" (Proverbs 16:18). The apostle Peter advises believers to clothe themselves "with humility toward one another, because God opposes the proud, but shows favor to the humble" (1 Peter 5:5).

Pride was the cause of Satan's fall from grace. He became consumed by pride due to his beauty and wisdom, desiring to be equal to or even above God (Isaiah 14:12–14). This desire led to his rebellion and subsequent expulsion from heaven (Revelation 12:7–9). A lot of people in the church struggle with pride. We see it regularly. It's part of the reason so many people have church hurt. Christians judging others because they think they sin less than someone else, pastors asking for money and showing up in flashy cars, churches turning away LGBTQ people, the list goes on. The root of this is pride.

When we read lists of sins, it's common to think of other people instead of yourself. It's hard to look inward, but it's worth the freedom you receive when you do. So many times pride got in the way of God's provision for me. Whether it was thinking I was too good to listen to someone's advice or making someone else feel bad because of my judgments, pride stood in the way of my progress of my becoming more like Christ. I have to check myself often.

One of the ways I catch myself being prideful is when I gossip about how someone else is dealing with a situation because I think I could handle it better. It's astonishing how quickly I can forget what God did in my life. I used to live out of my car and was addicted to meth for crying out loud! Another area of prideful behavior I struggle with is when someone isn't acting the way I want them to act. I give them the silent treatment because I believe I'm right and they're wrong. I know better now, so I don't do that very often anymore, but the urge is still there. Pride can make me feel like I fixed my own life, when

God gave me grace, and that grace is available to everyone. Not just me.

Journal Prompt

Dear God,

One area I have been prideful is _____. This may have made others feel _____. This is affecting me by _____. Will you help me start over tomorrow and do better?

Provision

Day 20

Sharing with Others

"In the same way, let your light shine before others,
that they may see your good deeds and glorify
your Father in heaven."

Matthew 5:16

The word *testimony* is in the Bible 175 times because it's our sharing with others what he does for us in our lives is important to God. I missed the mark with this. I didn't want to be too open about my faith and be seen as a Bible-thumper even though I knew God was the one that brought me out of everything.

Not sharing my testimony was selfish, because God did what he did for me so he could be glorified and help other people see what is possible. I wanted to keep all of my "hearing God" stories to myself so I didn't have to deal with naysayers or people expecting too much from me. I really wanted to blend in and become successful without promoting God, so I didn't have to deal with what comes with walking the Christian walk publicly. There is a lot of pressure to not be caught doing anything that could even seem immoral.

When I told the world I was sober, I knew that would put me in a position where people expected me to no longer drink alcohol at events. I needed that accountability to stay alive, and stop getting arrested. Being public about your sin takes accountability to a different level. It took me five years of asking God for help to get to the point where I could do this.

Writing about my experience has been a supernatural endeavor. Anyone that knows me knows that I'm in bed very early and I don't really work after the sun goes down, yet God gave me the strength to stay up late and write my testimony. He allowed the Scriptures that apply to everything I'm writing just naturally pop into my head. It's important to read the Bible, because when you are in a time of need, you will remember the Scriptures that apply to your circumstances. The Word of God is "alive and active. Sharper than any double-edged sword" (Hebrews 4:12). See, God is working in my life, and He's doing it because He is using me to share my testimony with you.

Jesus told a man he had healed to go home to his people and tell them how much the Lord has done for him and how he has shown him mercy (Mark 5:19). The woman at the well ran and told everyone about her encounter with Jesus (John 4:28–29). The Bible is made up of testimonies from people from thousands of years ago sharing their experiences with God so that God would be glorified, and we would seek our own experiences to believe. "Jesus Christ is the same yesterday and today and forever" (Hebrews 13:8). God is unchanging. If God used people to share their testimonies back then, why wouldn't he now?

Journal Prompt

Dear God,

Do I have a testimony to share? If I do, will you please help me share how you have worked in my life to bring me to where I am today? Right now, you are putting on my heart that my testimony will be _____.

Day 21

Provision Is Peace

"Peace I leave with you; my peace I give you.
I do not give to you as the world gives. Do not let your
hearts be troubled and do not be afraid."

John 14:27

When we pray for provision, often we are thinking of financial blessings or favor for a certain situation in which we want God's help getting what we want. I have learned that provision can simply be peace.

I have already mentioned that before I was saved, I wasn't interested in anything that felt slow or calm. I couldn't relate to the psalm that says, "He leads me by quiet waters" (Psalm 23:2). I thrived on the rapids of life. I realize now it was because I wasn't comfortable in my own skin. I didn't know how to be at peace, because I couldn't quiet the noise in my mind. Have you ever heard the phrase "It worked until it didn't"? That's what chaos was for me. It worked until it didn't.

For a while, toxic relationships worked for me because I could avoid the quiet that came with peace. I was able to always focus my attention on someone else instead of myself. If I was dating someone that I could try to fix, then I could focus on their problems instead of my own. I was afraid of working on myself.

This codependent behavior stemmed from the chaos I experienced in childhood. My dad was my first love and the example I had for what a man should be. Although my dad was a great dad for a long time, he made some big mistakes, and it caused a lot of drama for the family.

I've had conversations with hundreds, if not thousands of people who have experienced trauma, and it affects the way they make decisions, choose their partners, or deal with situations. It is very important to recognize how your experiences from the past have caused you to walk through doors that weren't meant for you. For me, my trauma affected me the most when it came to relationships.

When I met Ben, he hadn't been in a relationship for ten years, but God somehow gave him the patience to deal with me. One time he got us a season pass to six flags, so once a month we could give my nervous system some excitement by riding roller coasters. He also started planning spontaneous dates and surprising me so I could learn a healthy way of having a boyfriend that is unpredictable—as opposed to getting cheated on or abused.

As time went on, I began to really enjoy the still waters and feeling of peace. Now, I love my predictable and dependable boyfriend that I know I can count on. I am so grateful that God kept me on the right path while he worked on my heart and helped Ben help me. God gave me the strength and guidance I needed to support him as well. (Ben had his stuff to work on, too.) I can say with certainty that God used us to make each other better, which is how relationships are intended to be.

Psalm 23 goes on to say that God makes us lie in green pastures, he leads us to still waters. He restores our soul, and leads us into the paths of righteousness for his name's sake (Psalm 23:2–3). There were times that I felt like God was making me do stuff I didn't want to do, but I trusted that He was *making* me lie in green pastures despite my fear of boredom and discomfort. Surrendering my relationship with Ben to God and asking for his help certainly made me feel like God led me into paths of righteousness.

It turns out still waters aren't boring at all once you experience the provision that peace has to offer. My life is more abundant and exciting than it's ever been. I have no lack of spontaneity or surprises living for God. In fact, it's only because of Ben's support—managing my business and watching my dog—that I was able to take the time to write this book. This relationship has taken me to a new level because of the way I've been loved. I never had a relationship that actually made me better. The way your spouse loves you can either lift you up or tear you down. I'm grateful God brought me someone that would lift me up, even when I didn't want it. God is constantly surprising me and He makes my life more adventurous than I ever could imagine making for myself. Thank you, God, for making me lie in green pastures and leading me to still waters.

If you have been praying for a relationship that makes you feel better, and takes you to a new level, humble yourself before God and don't be afraid of the still waters. They aren't boring; instead, they bring peace and contentment.

Journal Prompt

Dear God,

The still waters I've been avoiding in my life are _____.
I have to let go of _____ so I can experience your peaceful provision. Please help me see what it looks like to let go and just be.

Day 22

Provision Is Protection

*"Be alert and of sober mind. Your enemy the devil
prowls around like a roaring lion looking
for someone to devour."*

— 1 Peter 5:8

Today's verse is one I keep in the forefront of my mind to protect my sobriety. It encourages believers to be vigilant and to be sober because the enemy is prowling like a lion, seeking whom he can devour. God knows this and does not allow us to be tempted beyond what we are able (1 Corinthians 10:13). We hear people say all the time "God won't give you more than you can handle." I always interpreted that as: God won't allow my business to get bigger than I can handle or this lawsuit won't be bigger than what I can deal with. Now that I have grown spiritually, God has revealed to me that I had the wrong thinking.

The truth is, my business will be bigger than I can handle and the lawsuit will be bigger than I can handle because I shouldn't be attempting to do life without God's help. I need God in everything I do. I need God to wake me up, to get me out of bed, to brush my teeth. I need God to allow my car to start. Everything is more than I can handle. So what does not being given more than we can handle really mean? Well, the apostle Paul explains it when he writes, "when you are tempted,

[God] will also provide a way out so that you can endure it" (1 Corinthians 10:13).

The "way out" is a text message at the right time, a song on your playlist, a moment to pause before making a bad decision, a conviction in your heart from the Holy Spirit. All these are examples of God's provision. Provision can simply be God providing a life raft before you jump off the deep end. His Word promises that when we are tempted, He will provide a way out. Knowing this has helped me notice the loving ways God throws curve balls for my benefit as well as appreciate them as they come. We are to humble ourselves "under God's mighty hand , that he may lift you up in due time" (1 Peter 5:6).

Over the years, I have learned that when I go to God with humility and admit my failures, He lifts me up. Like I've said before, I'm not perfect, and I don't strive to be, because I know that's not possible. I do try my best to be a better version of myself every day, and that includes confessing my pride to God on a daily basis so I can receive his help to be humble. There are so many ways that God offered me a way out of a situation, but I didn't take it. There are also times I did take the way out and was grateful for the life raft that saved me from my own mistakes.

One way God has done a great job intervening for me is when hiring people or signing on a new client. Usually, God will show me something right in the nick of time, so I can change my mind and not move forward. Sometimes, God takes care of stuff himself and intervenes. Jesus says that He cuts off every branch in him "that bears no fruit, while every branch that does bear fruit he prunes so that it will be even more fruitful." (John 15:2). Sometimes I hear Christians quote this verse to avoid accountability when people walk out of their lives. We have to always be willing to look at ourselves and take inventory of our own behaviors when relationships end or doors close. If we always just chalk it up to, "Well, Jesus pruned the vine!" then we don't grow. We have to be careful not to take Scripture out of context. This Scripture is part of the bigger picture where Jeus is using the metaphor of a vine and its branches to describe his relationship with his followers and the importance of remaining connected to Him for spiritual growth and fruitfulness.

One of the scriptures that I hear misused all the time is when people say money is the root of all evil. The Bible does not say that. Instead, it says, "The love of money is a root of all kinds of evil" (1 Timothy 6:10). It's not the money itself that is evil, but the *love* of money and the actions it can motivate is the root of all kinds of evil. We discussed this in Day 18, where we saw that we can't serve two masters.

Money should be viewed as a tool, and it can help you help a lot of people. Money can also cause a lot of problems. The bank accounts of two different people with the same amount of money look the same, but their souls could look very different. One could be worshiping God and the other worshiping money. Financial wealth can bring out the best or the worst in people. We see examples of this in our country every single day.

One thing that is hard to grasp is that sometimes God could be giving you provision of protection by not giving you money. Yeah, you read that right. It could be a gift that you haven't received the financial blessing you've prayed for. Jesus says, "it's easier for a camel to go through the eye of a needle, than for a rich man to enter into the kingdom of God" (Matthew 19:24). This means that when people have a lot of wealth and possessions, they are less likely to put their faith in God. Think about it. When do you tend to pray to God the most? Usually in a time of need, right? If you didn't have very many times of need, it's a lot harder to cultivate that relationship with God than if you are consistently leaning on God for help.

For many years I was in desperate situations, many of which included not having money. There are times I can look back and see that God didn't give me the money I was asking for, and I'm glad! Had he given me what I wanted before I was ready for it, I would've lost it because I wasn't ready to be a wise steward with what he wanted to bless me with. Now, I am at a place in my relationship with God that I know I need Him every single day to do anything.

Perhaps God knows that you wouldn't be leaning on him and building a relationship with him if you came into the money you're asking for right now. Remember, God wants you to have the desires of your heart, but the desires of your heart have to align with His will for your life. If you aren't in alignment with God, provision could look like protection, so you don't get too off track. I know it's not easy, but I would take gaining a deep relationship with God over instant gratification any day now that I know what God has to offer.

Journal Prompt

Dear God,

Perhaps you haven't given me _____ yet because you are helping me become better, so I don't lose it. Thank you for providing your provision with your protection. Please help me trust that you will provide whatever I need while I wait on you.

Day 23

Habits That Hold You Back

"You were taught, with regard to your former way of life, to put off your old self, which is being corrupted by its deceitful desires; to be made new in the attitude of your minds; and to put on the new self, created to be like God in true righteousness and holiness."

Ephesians 4:22–24

I've built a lot of really bad habits over the years. It's a lot easier to fall into bad habits than it is to create good habits, but it's a harder life to live with bad habits. The consequences of our actions can make everything more difficult. Yes, it's difficult to do the right thing, but in the long run it's even harder when you do the wrong thing. For instance, diet and exercise is not easy, but it's a lot harder to live with diabetes. Choosing to stay sober is hard, but getting arrested for a DWI sure does make things hard as well.

Today, I want you to take inventory of your habits. What are some habits that are holding you back from reaching your goals? What is a habit that you have tried time and time again to quit, but you can't seem to? I'm not talking about small indulgences like eating ice cream. Which by the way, is very hard for me, especially if it's a butter pecan ice cream cone! I'm talking about habits that negatively affect our health or keep us from living the life God intended for us.

A lot of people struggle with escapist behaviors to avoid doing hard stuff. This could be porn, video games, binge watching TV, or doom scrolling social media. I personally have workaholism issues, those things aren't something I struggle with as much, but what I do struggle with are destructive behaviors, such as using drugs and alcohol, disordered eating, or engaging in dangerous situations.

Whether binge-watching a series or getting drunk at a bar, these behaviors serve the same purpose: to escape. I am not suggesting that we never cut loose or relax. That's something I'm trying to do a better job at. If I am not producing, I struggle to see myself as worthy, but I know that's not true. We are human beings not human doings. However, when we are engaging in behaviors that harm us in order to check out, that's not going to help us reach our God-given potential.

For me, I have had to discover ways I could take a step away from reality that weren't harmful to me or others. Some of those activities include skating, dressing up in costumes, exploring nature, going to amusement parks, doing crafts, and playing with my dog. I once had to write down a list of things I like to do in case I had the itch to drink. When I got the urge to drink, I'd open up that list and do one of those things first. That has helped me stay sober.

You may have heard that it only takes twenty-one days to make or break a habit. Probably some motivational speaker came up with that to get people to think they could get results quick. The truth is that it varies from person to person. According to Jocelyn Solis-Moreira in "How Long Does It Really Take to Form a Habit?" a 2024 article in *Scientific American*, "a hallmark 2009 study on habit creation found that habits developed in a range of 18 to 254 days; participants reported taking an average of about 66 days to reliably incorporate one of three new daily activities. For me, it's way past the 250 days mark. Honestly, I would say it takes me about two years for a behavior to stick around. Looking back at my journal entries, anytime I wrote about a major change in my life, it was a two-year journey of wrestling with God to commit to the change. What habits are holding you back from your potential?

Journal Prompt

Dear God,

You know I really want to quit _____, but I lack the discipline. Can you please help me do one thing today that will jump start a new beginning for me? That one thing I feel like you are telling me to do is _____.

Day 24

Using God's Tools

"For it is God who works in you to will and to act
in order to fulfill his good purpose."

Philippians 2:13

One day I was praying for favor for Cornbread Hustle, and God told me I already had the tools I needed to help our company grow. I wrote down a list of all the tools and connections I already had. As I analyzed this list, I couldn't quite figure out what he wanted me to do. I felt like I was doing everything I could with the gifts he gave me. That's when God reminded me that I was relying on my own strength and not on Him.

We are told to "trust in the Lord with all of your heart and lean not on your own understanding" (Proverbs 3:5). What a conundrum I was facing. God was telling me that the tools I needed were already in my hands, yet Scripture tells me not to lean on my own understanding and trust the Lord. This is growth area for me. As someone who struggles with workaholism, I fall into the trap of leaning into my own understanding often. I take a lot of pride in my creativity and strategy when it comes to entrepreneurial projects. When God told me I already had all the tools I needed in my hands, He didn't mean my own abilities. He was talking about His.

One of the verses that I have misused a lot for my own benefit is "Faith without works is dead" (James 2:26 kjv). If I had a dime for every time I said this, I probably would have a million dollars. I will normally say this when someone is praying for something to happen for their career or their business to remind them that they can't just pray for help and receive it. I am writing today to tell you that I have been wrong. Sure, we want to have goals and work toward them, but that's not what this verse is about. This verse is emphasizing that true faith should be accompanied by actions and visible expressions of that belief. Working hard to make sure your company succeeds is not living out that belief, in fact it's the opposite.

If I stay up all night trying to fix my company on my own with my own ideas, that is not faith. That's simply works. If I continuously pray for God to bless my company, yet I'm not being obedient to living my faith out by helping others, that's simply faith. The two must work together. James goes on to say that "You believe that there is one God. Good! Even the demons believe that—and shudder" (James 2:19), so belief is not enough. It's our faith in action that makes our belief come to life.

God was right. I do have the tools in my hand that I need to help my company succeed. Those tools are my belief and my action working together simultaneously. What does belief in action look like? This is different for everyone because we are all unique. We all have different gifts. We are all "fearfully and wonderfully made" (Psalm 139:14).

Throughout each day we could miss the mark combining our faith and works. Maybe we pray for someone in need instead of providing help. Maybe you aren't tithing to the church because trusting God with your money is where your faith ends and your own works step in. Perhaps you know something you own would benefit someone else more, but you don't want to give it to them. There are moments throughout my entire day that I have to ask myself if I'm combining my faith and works or if I'm just letting one of them work independently because of my own selfishness or discomfort.

When you trust God, and I mean really trust God, it's easier to allow your gifts, money, and possessions to flow through your open hands because you know that God will replace it, and it's not your concern what happens with the gift you gave. Please know that I fail at this a lot of the time, but I'm striving to do better.

Before I make decisions on what actions to take is I ask myself, Is this coming from a place of fear or pride? If the answer is either one of those, I know I need to take my time and pray about it. The opposite of pride is humility, and the opposite of fear is love. Am I doing something out of love and humility? If the answer is yes, it's going to work out, if it's in God's will. It may not always feel like it, but God will work it out. I can say that with confidence because I have evidence. I can go back through these journals and see time after time when I did something out of love that seemed wrong by conventional standards. Every time, though, God made it right and provided for me.

One of the ways I am working to combine my faith and works right now is by writing this book. God has definitely given me the words to write this. It's not by my own works, but I am living out my faith by taking action and being obedient to what God is telling me to do. Making the decision to come out to this bungalow to write this book is definitely an act of humility and love for me. I am living out my love for you and God enough to share some very humbling events that took place in my life. This is how I'm using the tools in my hand that God gave me to combine my faith and works to live out my belief in action. What are some ways you can combine faith and works in your life right now?

Journal Prompt

Dear God,

Between the two: Faith and works, I have been more likely to lean on faith or works (circle one). Today, I would like to hear from you on what it looks like for me to combine the two. Lord, please help me have the faith to live out my belief in action. Search my heart and look for my fears and prideful thoughts so you can reveal them to me.

Day 25

He Restores My Soul

*"He restores my soul; He leads me in the paths
of righteousness For His name's sake."*

Psalm 23:3

What does it mean to have your soul restored? It's really hard to imagine until you experience it. When you are walking with God, you don't just experience it one time. For me, God restores my soul every time I come to Him for help. Sometimes my soul feels restored after a morning of being with Him in His word. There are those major events, though, where God really did a miraculous change in my life after I gave up and entered into a difficult surrender.

You've already read about the two biggest surrenders in my life: getting sober and getting on medication. Another way God is restoring my soul is through my relationship with Ben. Your soul becoming restored isn't something that happens with the snap of your fingers. Sometimes it can be that way if God wants it to be. I have heard stories from many people in prison about how God completely changed them in one single moment. It has never worked that way for me. I'm stubborn. God gives me opportunities, people, signs, and nature to talk to me while I'm kicking and screaming and not wanting to change.

I can look back and see that He was restoring my soul before I even recognized it. That's why I named my dog Love Story. I felt like God used her to reveal His nature to me. Later I realized

He was working to restore my soul before it got crushed. Let me explain.

It was around my birthday in January 2021. I was out with one of my girlfriends, and at the last minute we decided to change the restaurant where we planned to eat. We picked a place with a patio and updated each other on our lives. I had confessed to her that I really wanted a third dog, but I knew it was the last thing I needed because I already had two senior dogs that were a lot of work. She challenged me by saying, "Who cares, why don't you just get the dog if you want it?"

"Listen, the only way I'm getting a dog is if it falls in my lap, and it's free," I said.

In that moment, a lady walked by holding a dog and my friend waves at the lady and says, "Awww! I love your dog!"

"You want one?' she replied. "Because I own a shelter and have a one-eyed dachshund looking for a home. I can't stand how lonely she looks, so I'll waive the adoption fee if you want her." My friend was ecstatic shouting at me to get the dog, because it was a sign. I told the lady I would think about it and asked for her business card. My friend continued to work on convincing me throughout our brunch date, but I was firm on the decision that I wouldn't get the dog.

As we were pulling out of the parking lot, we saw a different lady walking her dog on the sidewalk. Want to guess what kind of dog? It was a one-eyed dachshund. That was enough for me. I could no longer ignore the spiritual nudge from God. We drove straight to the shelter, and I adopted Love Story.

I didn't know it at the time, but a few months later I would be grieving a major loss. I needed comfort and unconditional love. Love Story is a lap dog, and she was exactly what I needed. I also didn't know that Love Story would end up becoming part of my virtual twelve-week Starting Over program that people in prison view using tables. Love Story provided the residents with a virtual fury companion.

God knew what I needed before I needed it. He always does. I'm so glad I was obedient, because God provided me with a love story that restores my soul each and every day.

Many people have mentioned to me that they are envious of the way God speaks to me or shows me signs. I believe everyone receives these kinds of signs; it just takes practice listening and acting. I could've never had this love story to share had I not acted. I have so much practice stepping out in faith that I see signs quickly and try to be obedient no matter the discomfort.

God restores my soul as I'm faithful and obedient to follow His will. Take the time to spend with Him and allow him to restore your soul. God restores your soul by renewing, refreshing and guiding individuals toward righteous paths.

While it's not easy to walk in the paths of righteousness, it is the road that will lead you back to how God created you and how to find your God-given gifts and potential. Provision is God restoring your soul. All the other stuff doesn't really matter; it's just little God winks and gifts God gives us, so we can share our testimonies with others and build His kingdom for His glory.

Journal Prompt

Dear God,

I feel like I have noticed signs to do _____. Can you give me clarification? Can you help me feel what it's like to have my soul restored in this moment and for the days to come?

Day 26

Provision Is People

"As iron sharpens iron,
so one person sharpens another."

Proverbs 27:17

Isolation is where the devil wants you. When I was younger, my dad always said, "An idle mind is a devil's playground." It was a family rule that we were in at least one sport or some kind of activity. Idleness is not necessarily the absence of activity, but it is the presence of aimless activity. Idleness isn't doing nothing, but it's being busy doing the wrong things.

The apostle Paul said, "We hear that there are some among you who are idle and disruptive. They are not busy; they are busybodies" (2 Thessalonians 3:11). A lot of aimless activities include some of the isolating habits I pointed out earlier in this book: porn, video gaming, doom scrolling, and binge-watching Netflix. Before I quit drinking, I was aimless. I picked friends who would sit with me and drink and just talk about nonsense. If I could go back in time and have all the hours back that I spent in aimless conversations, I'd add so many more years to my life to live for Jesus. As much as I would like to change the past though, I can't deny that it hasn't brought me to where I'm at right now, writing this book.

One of the ways that God provides for us is through people. This is why Satan loves to isolate people. When you are isolated, Satan can put ideas into your head and make you believe them until you find yourself wondering why you're depressed and anxious and with no community. This definitely happened to me in my last days of drinking. I had gotten to a point where my only friend was alcohol. Exactly where the devil wanted me: alone, sad, and afraid. Without people pouring into me, I was not able to come out of the pit I was in. If God didn't think people and community were important, he wouldn't encourage us to use our gifts for other believers.

When I had just hit one year sober, I decided to be obedient to what God wanted me to do and planned a sober New Year's Eve party. I was afraid to take this step of faith because I had no money to ensure stuff got paid for if I didn't sell tickets or get sponsorships. I had no idea if there were enough people like me who wanted to celebrate without alcohol. Prior to promoting the event and doing all of the PR for it, I had pitched a company to sponsor the event for five thousand dollars. That's how much the venue cost and the exact amount I had left in my bank account, so I was so thankful that sponsor took care of that cost and paid the venue directly.

The morning of the party, I got a call from the venue saying the credit card charges were reversed. I couldn't believe it! I felt so betrayed. After I had already promoted the company on the news and put their logo on everything, they reversed the charges. In their defense, an agreement was never signed, but the marketing person that worked for them moved forward with me via a handshake deal and paid the venue so that was proof enough for me.

At the time, I didn't even have a couch in my living room because I was just getting back on my feet. All I had was a lawn chair. I paced around the lawn chair so much that morning that I could've created a hole in the hardwood floor. My anxiety was at an all-time high, and I was fuming mad. Nobody from the company that sponsored the event would answer my calls. I couldn't cancel because I already used that ticket money to pay for things like the photo booth, food, and entertainment. I used the only money I had to my name to pay for the venue. It was New Year's Eve, which means rent was going to be due in the next couple of days. How was I going to pay my bills? Was I going to lose the apartment I had just moved into? This was a terrible situation for me, and I didn't know how God was going to fix this one. In fact, I didn't trust He would.

Despite my angst and loss of money, the party was a hit. It was sold out, and it was a beautiful time. I was so proud that I had hosted a party that allowed people in recovery to have a great New Year's Eve without temptation. The next morning, however, was rough. Although I didn't suffer from a hangover, I felt like I did. What was I going to do without a penny to my name? I was still in that season where I didn't have many people in my life, and nobody I could ask for money. That's when God came through.

A woman I didn't know, and whose feed I've never seen again, sent me a message through Facebook Messenger: *Hi, I just wanted to let you know that your story has helped me quit drinking. I want to donate to your organization as a way to say thank you.* I responded that we are not a nonprofit, so we do not accept donations. She told me it was fine and that she wanted to give me a gift and to please just accept it because she felt led to do it. She asked me for my routing and checking account number, so I gave it to her. I expected there to be a twenty-dollar thank you gift in my bank account the next day. When I checked my account for the next couple of days and nothing showed up, I got scared that I had been scammed. I called the woman through Facebook Messenger. I asked her if it was really her that asked for my routing and checking information. She said it was really her and to just keep checking. The next morning there was a deposit there for five thousand dollars. I couldn't believe it. All good things come from God and God will work all things together for the good of those who love him and are called according to his purpose.

Even though Satan tried to get me to quit, God stepped in and showed me I could trust Him to fight my battles. What a gift! That was definitely one of those times my soul felt restored and my faith renewed. It doesn't always happen that way, and I don't expect God to bless me with thousands of dollars every time I'm in trouble, but I do know I can count on Him to show me He's with me and working on my behalf. God will use anybody to speak to you or reveal Himself to you. This is why I'm such a huge proponent for community and relationships.

Journal Prompt

Dear God,

I feel like you're using _____ to speak to me or reveal yourself to me. Can you please bring me more people this week to show me what you want me to see?

People

Day 27

Divine Appointments

"Carry each other's burdens, and in this way
you will fulfill the law of Christ."

Galatians 6:2

I spent a lot of Sunday mornings going to church alone when I first got sober. I really wanted to get sober on my own and not ask anyone for help. If I could build businesses, then surely I could get sober, I thought. That was a prideful mindset that prevented me from receiving God's provision.

After I was about six months sober, I felt miserable. I asked people on Facebook if it was normal to have so much anxiety and what I could do about it. People suggested I join a twelve-step group and get into community. I thought I was too special, smart, and important to walk into any of those recovery rooms.

One morning, while I was sitting by myself at church, the Holy Spirit nudged me to go to the altar and ask for prayer. After I received prayer for my loneliness, a woman came up to me and introduced herself. I recognized her as the pastor's wife. I felt nervous talking to her because I didn't feel good enough to attend church. The funny thing is I felt too prideful to go to a recovery room. It's interesting to me how our brain will tell us lies to protect our pride or reaffirm our fears.

The pastor's wife asked if I knew anyone from church. I told her I come alone. She asked if I would like to be introduced to anyone. I told her I was six months sober and struggling with loneliness and being motivated to stay sober. She asked for my phone number and connected me with a person from their congregation who had been sober for many years. That woman text me back and let me know there was a group of women that got together three days a week at six in the morning to watch the sunrise. I was a morning person, so I thought that would be a nice way to start my day before work, and I was desperate. That divine appointment was how I got to know what I call my sober sunflower sisters.

These women helped me through every emotion I was feeling and taught me to not be ashamed of my past but to learn from it. They prayed for me and with me. I never had people in my life whose only motive was to see me heal. Although it sounds good, it doesn't mean I accepted it easily. I was used to transactional relationships, so I was constantly trying to pay these girls in exchange for them helping me stay sober and find God.

I will never forget the day we were in a cabin for a sober girls' retreat. They rolled me up into a blanket like a burrito and told me to accept the love they are giving me and to stop trying to earn it. I was so embarrassed. I couldn't stop crying. I couldn't figure out if I was crying because of my embarrassment or my gratitude. God sent me people to show me what unconditional love looks like.

In the past, I had learned that love was transactional, but these women showed me that with the right people, it's not at all. Learning how to accept friendships without transactions has been a difficult journey for me, one that God has to restore one small step at a time. I have friends today that still have to remind me that they don't need anything from me except my time.

The sober sunflower sisters will forever be a pillar for my recovery. If you're wondering why I call them sober sunflower sisters, it's because during those dark times in my life, I had read somewhere that sunflowers turn and face each other for energy after the sun goes down. That's exactly what those women were to me: beautiful sunflowers willing to turn toward me when it became dark.

Journal Prompt

Dear God,

I need some light in my life. I feel like I have avoided seeking community by not _____. Please give me the courage to be obedient to walk into that field of sunflowers and find the ones that you planted for me.

Day 28

Miraculous Mentors

*"And the things you have heard me say in
the presence of many witnesses entrust to reliable people
who will also be qualified to teach others."*

2 Timothy 2:2

A woman sent me a message on LinkedIn: "I know this is really weird, and no obligation whatsoever, but God told me that I should mentor you and I'm just being obedient to that request." I looked at her profile and couldn't believe my eyes! She was the COO of a billion-dollar staffing company. Why on earth would I ever turn that down? This woman was humble enough to come to me with an offer that I shouldn't refuse, yet she respected the fact that I may think it's weird that she reached out. Wow!

It's been several years since that LinkedIn message, and this woman has been a light in my life, one of the people that God used the most to reveal Himself to me. Because of her, I try to do my best to dedicate my time mentoring others. There's a saying I hear in recovery rooms a lot related to helping others get sober: "I gotta give it away to keep it.". I think it works for just about anything in life we want to keep. Specifically, love.

This miraculous mentor of a woman flew me out to visit her home. She never once preached at me or told me what I needed to do to serve God. She glorified God by simply living out her beliefs. (Remember, faith without works is dead.) She not only had faith in God, but she lived out her belief through works by showing me the love that I needed. I was in a place in my life where I thought I had to be someone I wasn't in order to succeed.

This woman had Disney art all throughout her house. Her love for nostalgic Disney movies was prominent. I too love fun, whimsical things, but I had been trying to change into someone I'm not to appear more successful. She collected beautiful teapots, and she loved to host people in her beautiful home. She was truly an example of what it looks like to use the money God gives to bless others. She inspired me to live like Christ. I wanted to be like her. She took me to Disney World and showed me it was okay to have childlike wonder and be excited about life again.

As we swirled around and around in the teacups at Disney World, I could feel joy. I was laughing like a kid again and experiencing God in the best way. It still took me a lot of time to really experience joy on a consistent basis, because as I've mentioned, I would push away things God was giving me that could bring me joy to protect myself from pain. I didn't want to be disappointed. I was particularly afraid of people, because in the past, they caused me a lot of pain. That trip to see my mentor was another pillar for my recovery and pursuit to become more like Christ. She showed me what's possible and demonstrated a kind of love that is only possible with the power of the Holy Spirit.

Another mentor God sent me was a man that I had been doing PR for. He had written a book about workplace culture and was a successful entrepreneur that had sold his company for a lot of money. This was early in my career. It was after I got clean from meth, but also before I had ever shared publicly that I used to be addicted to drugs. I opened up to him a little bit and shared my story. He suggested that I visit the Prison

Entrepreneurship Program and volunteer my time by helping people in prison learn more about entrepreneurship. Fast-forward ten years, and my company has helped more than three thousand people find employment or become entrepreneurs after prison. God used one miraculous mentor to get the ball rolling for one of his purposes for me.

One other mentor I want to mention is a man that runs a successful truck repair company. He is a godly man that loves community and networking. Even though he was one of my paying clients, he had offered to mentor me because he loved what I was doing. I never turn down mentoring from people who have achieved more than I have, because I know I cannot do this without the help from God or the people He uses. He suggested that I join a Christian forum of twelve other business leaders who come together for a full day once a month. This entire day is made up of a Bible curriculum that aligns with running a business, as well as the opportunity for your peers to provide feedback or poke holes in ideas you have.

The major problem I saw with this is that it cost a lot of money to join. My pride was definitely getting in the way because I felt like I didn't need to "pay for friends," as I had put it. But God kept putting it on my heart to join and trust Him. I reached out to a forum organizer and told him I didn't need to be sold on it, and that I wanted to move forward.

When I showed up to the first meeting, it was me and a bunch of men. I felt extremely uncomfortable, and the last thing I wanted to do was pay money to spend time around men who I felt were pretending to be better men than what they really were. Up until then I had assumed that most men cheat on their wives. It was in that forum where I was able to see what a real man that loves God and his wife looks like. If it weren't for that community, I probably would've never been able to stay in a relationship with a good guy, because they helped me through all my fears and limiting beliefs around relationships.

As time went on, I met females in the group who became some of my best friends. I remember telling the forum organizer that what I wanted to get out of joining was friendship, because I wanted to find women who were also Christian business leaders to do life with. I remember it like yesterday. I told him, "If I were ever to get married, I don't have enough women in my life to have any bridesmaids."

Who are some mentors that changed the trajectory of your life? Perhaps they were just everyday people, and you are just now realizing they were in fact a miraculous mentor. Can you be that mentor to someone else?

Journal Prompt

Dear God,

I'm in need of a miraculous mentor. Can you please bring me a mentor to guide me in the direction you would like me to go? Right now, I'm heading toward _____ but I feel like you want to redirect me toward _____.

Day 29

Casting Stones

*"When they kept on questioning him,
he straightened up and said to them, 'Let any one
of you who is without sin be the first
to throw a stone at her.'"*

John 8:7

Jesus says, "Let him who is without sin among you be the first to throw a stone at her" (John 8:7 esv). He said this after an adulteress was caught in the act and the religious leaders of the day were testing Jesus. Jesus challenges hypocrisy and judgment.

I am just as guilty as anyone for casting judgment on others. I have to work really hard to try to view people the way God views them instead of projecting my own fears, desires, or insecurities onto them. When I judge people, it comes from a place of insecurity or fear. Sometimes, I'm projecting how I think I would do things differently if I were in their shoes. Regardless of the reason, it's wrong.

As Christians we are supposed to hold each other accountable, and we know that iron sharpens iron, but we can do it in a way that calls someone up instead of calling them out. I haven't always the best leader, friend, or mentor. Sometimes I would shame my workers, friends, or mentees by telling them what they should do. Yikes! I hate that in a position of leadership I could unintentionally harm others with my words because of my unwillingness to give myself grace or accept the grace God was giving me.

The toughest leaders you know are the ones who don't take any excuses and who usually haven't given themselves grace or accepted the grace God is giving them. If you have a boss who micro-manages or is constantly shaming people for their work, pray for them. Know that they are human too, and they need to experience God's grace in order to change.

I wasn't able to be a good leader until I started to reparent my inner child. I needed to provide the love, safety, guidance, and compassion that I lacked in childhood, by becoming my own internal caregiver. Now, when someone is really getting under my skin and I'm starting to judge them, I try to picture them standing there as a little boy or a little girl. This instantly helps me give them grace and pray for them. In the line of work I am in, I hear a lot of people cast stones at others. I'll hear someone in prison talking down on someone who is in prison for a sex offense when they are sitting in prison for murder. It's easy to want to look at someone else's sin and think yours isn't as bad as theirs, but the Bible says that all sins are equal in God's eyes.

That may sound like bad news to you, but it's actually good news. Why? Well, since every sin is equal, Jesus wiped away your sins as far as the east is from the west (Psalm 103:12) and that they shall become white as snow (Isaiah 1:18). It was hard for me to really believe my sins were removed, because I still face the consequences of my sins to this day. I have learned that while we will still face the consequences of our sins, we can be free from condemnation from them. God gives us a peace that surpasses all understanding (Philippians 4:7).

I can feel that peace as I read through some of the letters I wrote to God when I was in such pain and despair. I thought this would be a very emotional trip and a struggle to write this book, but reading the letters have brought me closer to God and helped me let go of more resentments. There were people that made me believe I was a hateful person who didn't care about anyone. Looking back at these letters, I see that I loved, and I loved hard. I just didn't know how to give it or receive it.

Now that I know that about myself, I'm even more equipped to give grace to others who may not know how to love me the way I need to be loved. I can't for the life of me figure out how I held onto over twenty years of journals from all the times I lived out of my car, moved, or couch surfed. Through fifteen years of addiction to drugs and alcohol, I still had my journals that kept me close to God. He knew before I knew that I would be writing this book one day and He gave me a desire to hold on to these memories, even though some of them are very painful. I can read through these journals and see that I hurt just as many people that hurt me. It was clear I didn't know my behavior was causing harm to others, and I was more focused on being the victim while I cast stones.

Are there people you feel convicted for judging? Can you be objective and take a look at the judgement and see how it fits into your own fears or insecurities?

Journal Prompt

Dear God,

I do not want to be a judgmental person. I feel convicted for judging _____, and I need your help to remove this judgment from me, because I cannot do it on my own. Lord, please help me see others through your eyes instead of my own.

Day 30

Remembering Rejections

*"If the world hates you, keep in mind that
it hated me first."*

John 15:18

The more people we interact with, the more we are at risk for rejection. I don't care who you are, nobody likes to feel rejected. Rejection can come in all forms: not getting the job, not being accepted in a social setting, being bullied or ridiculed, trolls on social media making comments on your posts, being dumped, and sometimes we even feel rejected by our own family members. Those last two stung a little when I typed them. My most painful rejections were by a boy, followed by my father.

As I read through letters from middle school, I see that I felt rejected a lot for my quirkiness and assertiveness. I always wanted the cute, popular boys to be interested in me, but I somehow would always settle for the kids that would get in trouble. I became one of those kids who got in trouble, so I could fit in and hang out with the boys. I was already smoking weed out of a Coke can and sneaking out with my parents' car when I was in middle school. I was such a rebellious preteen, and I was always looking for trouble. Trouble gave me a rush of excitement.

During the summer before high school, I met a boy. He was so dreamy. He had just moved to my neighborhood from across town. This was a guy I was willing to change for. He made me feel alive and happy. We spent time together every day that summer. It was just like the classic movie *Grease* where Sandy and Danny fall in love over the summer. Just like in the movie, it was all good until school started. You see, Mr. Dreamy was popular, and a good kid. He got to know *me* that summer not my reputation.

We started high school as a couple. It didn't take very long for him to become distant. I remember he knocked on my door one day after school and told me that he wanted to break up with me. He didn't have to tell me why. I already knew. He was nominated to be on the homecoming court, but I obviously didn't make the cut.

He handed me the mum his mom made for me and said he still wanted me to have it. I did my best to hold back my tears and told him I understood. He proceeded to tell me that his mom told him he had to stick with his commitment and take me to the homecoming dance and that he would be at my house Saturday to pick me up. That Saturday, I spent all day getting ready. Even though it was a bit of a pity date, I felt excited to go to the homecoming dance with Mr. Dreamy. I sat on my stairs and waited. And waited. And waited. An hour went by, and he never showed up. I ran to my room, threw off my heels, and cried in my navy blue dress that I was so excited to wear. My mom came up stairs and told me to stop crying and put on my shoes because I was going to the dance. "You're not going to let a boy ruin your fun night," she told me. "Get up, let's go."

My mom drove me to the homecoming dance herself. I remember it being so awkward because she was trying so hard not to cry. It kinda worked, because I didn't want to cry anymore because I didn't want her to cry. I can only imagine how hard she must have bawled seeing me walk into that school by myself in my dress and heels, almost two hours late.

I took a deep breath and walked in. Mr. Dreamy was standing in the corner with his group of jock friends. I stormed across the dance floor, tapped him on his shoulder, and said "Hey!" He turned around and nervously laughed at me because his friends were there. "You forgot to pick me up. But I made it. I'm here." And then I walked off.

That moment was so painful, I buried it so deep I didn't remember it until I had to do the hard work of healing when I finally met Ben. My pattern of sabotage with men started at that point in time because I never wanted to be rejected again.

My second major rejection came from my father. Growing up my dad and I were like best friends. We used to listen to Madonna all the time in the car and sing along. He used to test my knowledge of football teams and the cities they belonged to. He would yell out a city, and I would respond with the football team that belonged to that city. My dad was a die-hard football fan. He was a referee, so he always wanted to teach me about football. I didn't care what my dad wanted to teach me as long as I was spending time with him.

One of my favorite things to do with him was go on eighteen-hour-long road trips to his hometown in West Virginia. There was nothing like that cold breeze coming through my dad's window as he stuck out his hand and felt the crisp air. Tears would always roll down his cheek when he drove into his hometown because when he was sixteen years old, he found his dad dead, by suicide. My dad never did the work to heal from that, and it became trauma that got passed down a generation.

Another thing I loved to do with my dad is sit in the garage with him while he changed the oil in the car. We would strategize and plan pranks we could play on other family members. I also loved doing all the things with my dad most daughters probably have no interest in doing: going to Auto Zone, Home Depot, Wal-Mart, literally I would go anywhere just to be able to hang out with my dad. Around the same time I got rejected by Mr. Dreamy, my dad started drifting away, and I started seeing less and less of him. When I did see him, he was in a really bad mood. Sometimes it would get scary, and I would be afraid of him. No man has ever broken my heart the way my dad did. It was easy for me to get over any boy from school, but I was never going to get over my dad.

Before you judge my parents, just know that they did everything they could to get me to change my behavior. I can't count the number of times I got grounded, how many times my mom made me watch *It's a wonderful life* so I would learn how to be grateful, and the number of times my dad made me watch *The Ten Commandments* so I would get scared into following some set of religious rules. It got to a point where they didn't know what to do anymore and were facing their own battles, so I had even more freedom to cause trouble. My parents did the best they could with the cards they were dealt in life. They didn't do the work I have been able to do on myself, so some generational cycles were certainly passed down. Are there any rejections you've buried that came up for you while reading this?

Journal Prompt

Dear God,

A rejection that has shaped the way I am today is _____. I ask that you help me take some time to grieve this rejection and heal from it. Help me reparent my inner child today.

Day 31

Realizing Resentments

"Get rid of all bitterness, rage and anger, brawling and slander, along with every form of malice. Be kind and compassionate to one another, forgiving each other, just as in Christ God forgave you."

Ephesians 4:31–32

In recovery programs, it's often said that resentments are one of the top reasons for relapse. I can attest to how harmful resentments are. Not being able to set boundaries and holding onto resentments are a big reason for much of my drug and alcohol use. I have always struggled with being resentful. Like a bad habit, it got to a point where I didn't know how to live without resentments. As long as I could be resentful at someone else, I could avoid looking at myself. One of the first, and biggest resentments that was most difficult to move past was the resentment against my father. My hero. My protector. My one and only dad. He really let me down, and I went down as a result of it.

There was an older boy living across the street who had already dropped out of high school. He was definitely one of those bad kids, which was why I was hanging out with him. We were sitting in his bedroom one night, and I will never forget what he said. "You know your dad smokes, right?"

"Smokes!? He'd never smoke! He hates cigarettes!" I said.

He laughed and said, "Not cigarettes, Cheri!"

"Weed?" I said. "He's totally antidrug; he wouldn't do that."

He looked at me and said, "He smokes ice." I didn't know what that meant, so I asked what ice was. "It's meth. It's a drug that makes you stay up and lose weight and feel really productive." I remembered my dad telling us he took too many energy pills sometimes when he was being mean, but I never thought it was possible that he'd try drugs. My dad was such a straightlaced guy he wouldn't let me go to school on pajama day because he didn't want boys to see me in my pajamas. That was a dad that cared for me and loved me. I was in complete shock and disbelief.

"Cheri, look outside. It's eleven o'clock at night and your dad is mowing the lawn, in the rain. Normal people don't do that. Your dad's on meth." I asked him how he knew that for sure, and he replied, "Because I sell it to your dad."

Now I knew how I could get my dad's attention. I would become his drug dealer. The only problem is, I got addicted to it too. The first time I tried meth I actually hated it. I wrote in my journal that I couldn't wait to be able to go to sleep because I had been awake for almost three days. I had started to feel shaky and was hallucinating at school from lack of sleep.

In a notebook my friend and I wrote in, I told her about this drug that I tried and how much I hated it. I told her I wasn't going to ever do it again. A few pages later, I was hooked, and so was she, as well as several other high school girls I had introduced it to. I really didn't want to ever smoke meth again, but the come down was so bad that I felt like I needed the energy. So I got more. I did meth every day for two years after that.

This is when I learned all about transactional relationships. My dad would buy me booze and let me throw parties because he needed what I had to offer him. I would also get him to buy me new clothes from the mall or give me money whenever he felt bad for being mean. I learned how to manipulate his highs and lows from the drug, and I learned how to become valuable to him. One line neither of us could ever cross: we never used in front of each other. We both knew we couldn't handle it. We were both addicts who didn't want to live the life we were living, but we didn't know how to crawl out of the darkness the devil brought us into.

Are there any big resentments that have held you back from loving the way God intended you to love? Have resentments caused you to seek out transactional relationships?

Journal Prompt

Dear God,

One big resentment I'm still holding onto is _____. Please help me seek relationships that are loving and help me recognize if I have transactional relationships that are hindering my spiritual growth.

Day 32

Feeling Unworthy

"A good name is more desirable than great riches;
to be esteemed is better than silver or gold."

Proverbs 22:1

We need to acknowledge what we have believed about ourselves based on what we believe others think of us. I've lived most my adult life feeling embarrassed for the paths I took and the bad influence I was on others. This embarrassment served well when I would go into overdrive working hard to prove I wasn't a failure. This is one of those things that worked until it didn't, because like I said before, nothing can fill that God-sized hole in your heart but God.

It's easy to get caught up in what people think of you, especially when our entire lives are on display on social media. Facebook came out just as my class was graduating high school, so we had no chance to figure out adulthood without failing in front of the world. Unless you were one of those people who did a good job keeping your life private like my younger brother. He is a stud. He's always been better than me at just about everything. Whether it's corn hole or a game of Uno, he's going to win. I love my brother, and he's one of my most favorite people to hang out with. We stayed very close over the years because we share the same deep pain of losing our father to drugs. However, my brother also lost me to drugs there for a while. So did my mom.

When my mom and dad finally divorced, I made a pact with my brother. He would take care of Mom, and I'd take care of Dad. We cried and hugged and I said goodbye. Although my father and I only lived up the street, the distance was far because of the difference in lifestyles. My brother was going to college; he was a good kid with a normal life. My mom worked hard and provided a safe stable home for my brother. When I went to live with my dad, my mother did not know he was using drugs. It was so out of character for my dad to use drugs that nobody thought it was even a possibility. She figured he was cheating. She divorced him because we were getting evicted from our home, and she didn't understand why.

I always blamed my mom and brother for not coming to save me (even though I was the one who ran away). In reality, there was nothing they could've done. I was on meth and was going to do what I wanted. I always felt like such a black sheep, probably because I was arrested more times than I can count. Mostly for trivial stuff like unpaid tickets and petty crimes.

My reputation was so bad that when I got off meth, I still never felt good enough for my brother. I felt like I had to prove to him and everyone else in the family how successful I had become. What I didn't realize is they were tired of hearing about my company or my successes. I made it even worse for myself by working so hard to get their approval. Sometimes people aren't bragging, they're just seeking approval. When I see someone doing this, I meet them with love like the sober sunflower sisters did for me. My insecurities of becoming the black sheep of the family grew more and more as I continued to get into toxic relationships and find myself in bad situations.

In high school my first business was a photography business, so I was able to make money doing senior pictures for my peers. I did really well because the parents paid me a lot of extra money to use Photoshop to remove acne or braces.

Back then, we didn't have filters or AI. It actually took skill, and I could charge $250 for retouching a photo. Remember Mr. Dreamy? Well, his mom paid me to do his high school graduation photos. I wondered if he knew what had become of my life. We ended up working together at Blockbuster, and he gave me a very sincere apology and told me he never got over what he had done to me. I told him to let it go and that it was in the past. He told me he felt I was going down a really bad path and that I shouldn't be dating the guy I was dating at the time. My reputation preceded me, and I just wanted to disappear from shame and didn't want help from someone who had hurt me so badly.

Even though I was making money, it didn't take long for me to be evicted from my apartment, not because I couldn't pay but for smoking weed. Since the cops had to get involved, it got back to my cheerleading coach, and they decided to kick me off the squad. I was just grateful they didn't know what else I was using and selling. I moved into a budget suites and barely finished my senior year.

Because I missed so many days of school, I had to do community service to get my diploma. Even though I was struggling with meth addiction, I still made a point to complete the community service because I really didn't want to do nearly four years of high school and have nothing to show for it. It really wasn't a pretty sight. High on meth, folding clothes at the Goodwill.

There is a section in my yearbook of someone jokingly saying that the best part of the year was the "Cheri stories." It was an inside joke. They were making fun of all my stories because I was on meth going a hundred miles a minute telling outrageous stories during lunch in the cafeteria. I hold nothing against anyone who made fun of me or hurt me. The only reason I'm writing about it, is because I want to paint a picture of how our life experiences and rejections can change the way we live and how we think about ourselves and others.

Is there a season in your life that has made you feel less worthy? Do you fear people still remember you for who you were at a low point in your life? Sometimes I still struggle with this, but instead of searching for confidence, I seek GODfidence. This is knowing my identity in Christ and knowing how he sees me instead of how the world sees me (or saw me). Knowing where I come from made it really hard for me to have the confidence to write this book. My biggest fear was that people who knew me back then would laugh at me. I now know the people who knew me back then will instead see what God did in and through me. This is my testimony.

Journal Prompt

Dear God,

Lately I've been feeling unworthy because I feel like people have seen me as _____. Please help me see myself the way you see me, and give me the GODfidence that can only come from you.

Day 33

When We Cause Our Own Pain

"The LORD is close to the brokenhearted and saves those who are crushed in spirit."

Psalm 34:18

Pain is inevitable. Sometimes people hurt us, and they don't even mean to. How many times have you unintentionally hurt someone's feelings because of something you said? How many times have you been mad at someone and they didn't even know you were mad?

Things did get a lot worse for me, and I did some unthinkable things. One of the most unthinkable things I did was buy drugs from the same guy that I met at the pizza place where I worked, the one I mentioned in Day 14 who sexually assaulted me at that party. Being in the drug world, I ran into him and actually ended up inviting him into my motel room because I wanted drugs. He offered to pay my rent for that week. After I paid him for my drugs, I told him it was time to leave because I had company coming over. "I'm not leaving," he said. He laid his gun on the table and said, "This is my room for the week. I paid for it, and I'm going to use it." I told him he could have it and packed up all of my stuff in my car. This is where I ended up. I had just graduated high school, and I was living in my car. I thought to myself if I'm going to live in my car, I should at least enjoy the view. I drove to West Virginia because I missed my dad. We weren't talking, but maybe I could remember the good times and feel that crisp breeze come into my window.

I was more alone than I had ever been. I had nobody. I really didn't know what I was going to do when I got there. I just wanted to get away from where I was. It was the first time in my life I thought changing my environment would make things better for me, but they only got worse. On my way to West Virgina, I hit a deer in the middle of the night in Kentucky. It was a pitch black. I was on a winding road with no lights whatsoever. I had to get out and push my car into a ditch, because it was totaled. I waited on the side of the road for someone to come by. I saw headlights and jumped up and down, waving my arms. An eighteen-wheeler pulled over to the side of the road. I was petrified, because I had no cell service and only fifty dollars to my name. This was like the beginning of a horror movie like *Wrong Turn*. What else was I going to do though?

The man must have been hauling Marlboro cigarettes because he smoked a ton of them. He took me to a motel (if you can even call it that). It was the worst place I had ever seen. I contemplated just sleeping outside, but as a city girl, I was afraid to get eaten by a bear. I had two choices: sleep with roaches or get eaten by bear. I chose the roaches. I didn't get a wink of sleep, because I spent most the night high on meth, paranoid, shoving furniture against the door so nobody would break in to sexually assault me. To this day, I am in awe at God's protection over me that night. I'm grateful for that truck driver who dropped me off without making me his prey.

The next day, I called one of my dad's family members and borrowed money to take a bus all the way back to Texas. It was the hottest, most uncomfortable ride I've ever been on. It was also my first time to panhandle. I was so hungry I couldn't stand it, so I was asking other bus passengers for money. I remember one guy said, "Girl, it's just Arby's. What do you want? I'll buy it for you." I got the Arby's 5 for $5 and inhaled all five items I picked from the menu.

The pain people caused, particularly my dad, motivated me to make harmful and destructive decisions. I grew to hate myself so badly, that I purposely put myself in situations where I could get killed, so I didn't have to kill myself. The poems I wrote at that time reveal just how much I wanted to die. I came back home and tried to get sober because I was tired of living the way I was living.

My mom took me in and helped me get a car. I promised her that I wouldn't do any drugs, but I did slip up a couple of times. Eventually, I quit. One night I was up late, high on meth. A video of a church play popped up. There was someone in dark clothes dancing with the devil and losing themselves, but then they were dancing with Jesus and the black clothes fell off to reveal new white clothing. It made me want a new life. My mom enrolled me in online graphic design school, and I began to work on getting my life back. I recognized that people had caused me a lot of pain, but nobody caused me more pain than I had caused for myself.

Journal Prompt

Dear God,

People have caused me pain, but _____ has caused me the most pain. Please help me forgive them and myself for the decisions I've made or ways I've acted because of this hurt I endured.

Pain

Day 34

Pain Produces Endurance

"Not only so, but we also glory in our sufferings, because we know that suffering produces perseverance; perseverance, character; and character, hope. And hope does not put us to shame, because God's love has been poured out into our hearts through the Holy Spirit, who has been given to us."

Romans 5:3–5

Over the years, God has turned my pain to purpose. Even though I never smoked meth again after seeing that church video one night after moving in with my mom, I still struggled with earning approval from others. In order to forgive my father, I had to accept the fact that he could relapse and let me down again, and I expected it. It never hurt any less though.

By the time I got sober, my biggest dream was for him to get sober and come work with me at Cornbread Hustle, but things got worse before they got better, and history kind of repeated itself. This time because of alcohol. I wanted to run away. I was living out of my car and decided that I was going to go to Detroit and start over and open a Cornbread Hustle out there. Not only was it a massive failure, but my alcoholism also got worse, and I got arrested again!

I had accidentally driven across the Canadian border and asked to turn around. It seemed suspicious, especially with my Texas plates, so they asked to search my car. I had Adderall and guns. Turns out you can't just drive over the border with guns. Since I didn't have a prescription for Adderall, I was facing a possession of a controlled substance and gun charges. I could not believe it.

For the first time ever, I got arrested without even trying to get in trouble! It really made me feel like I had a bad streak I couldn't get rid of. Border Protection had really thought they made a big bust, though, because I had cases of cornbread mix in my car, and as a marketing gimmick, we wrapped them in kilo-sized packaging. They literally stripped my car looking for drugs. I kept telling them it was just cornbread mix because I was hustling and doing whatever it took to make money for our company. I would even set up at gas stations and make cornbread dessert treats and sell them.

I was never a bad person; I just had a hard life, and it broke me. Rebuilding from the brokenness was the bravest and hardest thing I had ever done in my life. That's why I love helping others do the same. I owe so much to God and his people for what he's done for me.

Miraculously, Border Protection ended up letting me go because the Detroit police didn't want to deal with me. I couldn't believe it. I did not expect to just drive away from there with no criminal charges. I'd have a hard time believing it today if I hadn't kept the documents that show the items they confiscated from me. The journals, letters, and documents that I've kept are how I can look back and see what God did for me when I couldn't help myself. I wish I could say that was my last arrest, but I had just one more when I got home from Detroit. It was the DWI that eventually led me to making that decision to get sober on Christmas morning of 2018.

Looking back at all this pain shows me what God can do and how He can turn our pain to purpose. There are so many times I've wondered why it needed to be like this, and I would be lying if I didn't feel sorry for myself at times. The biggest blessing I got out of all of this pain, though, is the way I hear from God. If I had to go through all of that to hear Him the way I hear him now, I'm okay with it. We are called to rejoice in our sufferings, knowing that "suffering produces perseverance, perseverance character, and character hope. And hope does not put us to shame, because God's love has been poured out into our hearts through the Holy Spirit, who has been given to us" (Romans 5:3–6).

Journal Prompt

Dear God,

Today I feel like you are telling me that You can turn my pain into purpose by _____.

Day 35

Painful Prayers

*"This is the confidence we have in approaching God:
that if we ask anything according to his will, he hears us."*

1 John 5:14

If you really trust God to answer your prayers, be prepared to have them answered painfully if that's in His will. I prayed so hard and so long that my dad would get sober. When I was around one year sober, my dad had to get emergency quadruple bypass. I became my dad's caretaker, and I got what I prayed for: a sober dad. Not only was he a sober dad, but he was also an emotional dad.

Anything and everything made him cry, and he was so proud of me. He thought I was the best person in this world, and he was my biggest cheerleader, always cheering me on from the hospital bed and watching our company on the news when we got news coverage. He would text all of his friends and tell them all about me. He would talk to everyone and anyone about me. My dad was my best friend. We shared a bond I can't explain. Yes, there was a trauma bond as well as codependency, but I loved my dad as the dad who sang all the Madonna songs with me. The dad that taught me the cities of each football team, and most of all the dad that loved me and always has loved me. There were just seasons in his life he was unable to love me the way I needed it, and that's okay because God stepped in and gave me what I needed to heal.

Over the next couple of years, I took care of my dad. I spent every day after work at his house. It was like God gave me exactly what I wanted. I got to spend time with my dad, and we were both sober. It was a dream come true! I was able to ask him questions and get closure. Our relationship got so tight. He did what he could to help me with Cornbread Hustle. He would buy spray bottles for us and allowed my team to set up a disinfectant dispenser in his back yard, so we could fill up our equipment when we were in that area. Nothing else really mattered to me. I had my dad back, and my company was thriving. God had answered my prayers.

Just as everything was going well, my dad had started going downhill pretty quickly. As he regained his strength after the surgery, he would push the limits and would go missing for a few days at a time. I would worry so much and be so angry at him for disappearing on me.

One day when we were at breakfast, I was so upset I told him he dresses like a homeless person and that I was embarrassed to be in public with him. I was angry at him because I knew he wasn't doing what he needed to do to maintain sobriety. We let it go because our food arrived at the table. He asked me to pray for him. He had never done that before. I prayed that God give him peace and take his addiction away and cure his mental health issues.

That evening, I was talking to a recovery coach, and she told me to picture my dad in a bubble, and let him float up to heaven to be in the care of God. She told me to ask God to take this from me, because it's been too much to bear. My dad had sent me a text that night inviting me over for pizza, but I told him no because I was just exhausted with emotions and dealing with him. That was our last text exchange. My father died that night. My best friend was gone.

After that, I stopped praying for several years. I still wrote my "dear God" journal entries, but I didn't ask for anything anymore. I decided if God is sovereign and going to decide what He's going to do anyways, then why even pray. I did have a relationship with God, and I knew that this was for the best, but knowing I prayed for it hurt so bad. "Though I walk through the valley of the shadow of death, I will fear no evil; For You are with me; Your rod and Your staff, they comfort me" (Psalm 23:4 nkjv).

God revealed Himself to me and gave me a lot of comfort through my grieving process. God waited to take my dad in a time in my life where I had the money to fly his body to West Virginia and bury him in the mountains. I buried him on April Fool's day, because there was a piece of me that really hoped he was just playing one of his pranks on everyone. After his funeral, I cleared everything out of his house, gutted it, and remodeled it. I live there now.

For about a year, I was my grandmother's caretaker until I could get her out to West Virginia with her family. God knew I would need her and that she would need me. We were like two peas in a pod. We went everywhere together and made funny videos and dressed up. The only way we could get through the grief was to laugh.

That year my company was scaling beyond what I could handle. It was very hard for me because grief took away a lot of my motivation because my number one cheerleader was now dead. I stayed sober, though, and God carried me through it all. God worked with me on the prayer thing and helped me understand that prayer is for strengthening our relationship.

Jesus tells us to "Ask and it will be given to you; seek, and you will find; knock, and the door will be opened to you. For everyone who asks receives; the one who seeks finds; and the one who knocks, the door will be opened" (Matthew 7:7–8).

I have always been really good at the seeking and knocking part. I'm a doer. What I have struggled with the most in my faith journey with is the asking part. Particularly because I was afraid of how God would answer my prayers after my father passed away, and I didn't want to be disappointed when prayers weren't answered. Now, I know that if God doesn't do it for me, or He says no, it's for the best. I trust Him like that. Before, it wasn't so easy. I was trying to have faith in God without trusting Him with my life. That was just about as miserable as trying to control my drinking. Eventually, I surrendered just like I did with the alcohol, and I decided to give my entire life to God. Not just some of it.

Was there ever a prayer you've been afraid to ask for? Has a prayer been answered in a way you don't like? Asking is the initial step of expressing a need or desire to God, seeking involves a more active and intentional effort to build a relationship with God, and knocking builds upon these actions by living out your belief in actionable, demonstrable ways, trusting that doors meant for you will open. Of the asking, seeking, and knocking what's been most difficult for you?

Journal Prompt

Dear God,

My prayer life lately has been _____. Today I feel like you're asking me to _____ so I can hear you better. Of the ask, seek, knock actions, I struggle the most with _____. Can you help me grow in this area?

Day 36

Full-Circle Events

"He has saved us and called us to a holy life—not because of anything we have done but because of his own purpose and grace. This grace was given us in Christ Jesus before the beginning of time."

2 Timothy 1:9

Remember those letters from jail I wrote my parents when I was fifteen that said I felt like God was telling me to come back and help people in jail one day? Well, after my dad passed away, as a way to process my grief, that's when I created the twelve-week Starting Over program to help people process their emotions and turn their pain into purpose. This program is currently being offered in the same jail where I wrote those letters. As of this writing, over two hundred residents have graduated from the program. This is how God makes beauty from ashes (Isaiah 61:3).

The junk hauling business I started, Junk Hustlers, is also a full circle event for me. Remember when I said that I emptied out my dad's house? He was a mild hoarder, so I had to rent a dumpster to get rid of everything. Going through stuff when you're grieving is not fun. I thought that maybe I could create a company that would help others when they are dealing with grief and cleaning out a mess.

At the time, I didn't know it would come full circle and become a pathway for real estate investments. Now we are turning hoarding houses into second chance rentals for people who have criminal records. In fact, my dad's house will soon become a second chance rental for someone. Another cool full-circle event is my very first recruiter for Cornbread Hustle runs the day-to-day operations for Junk Hustlers. He is also the COO for a construction building materials company, and they needed some additional ways to earn revenue. I decided to let my gifts flow through my hands and trust God to replace it later on. I gave all my junk hauling equipment to the building materials company, so they could grow the business and reap the rewards. I still own part of the company, but it's theirs as much as it's mine. Believe me when I say it was not easy for me to get to the point in my life where I could trust everything will just "work out." I make these decisions after a lot of prayer, and when I have total peace about something, I know God will work everything out regardless of how hard things get. The reason I can have faith like this is because as I look back at my journals, I see that everything did work out, and all my prayers were answered. My prayers weren't always answered the ways I wanted them to be, but they were answered the way I needed them to be.

There are a lot of full-circle moments that happen in my life, and I give God all the glory for it. I get to experience full-circle events on a regular basis at my company when we are able to help someone I once sold drugs to, did drugs with, or bought drugs from. I always thought that would be awkward, but it's not at all. It shows how great God is and how he is always in the business of setting up divine appointments and making all things right to help his children.

Writing this book is such full-circle moment. As I flip through thousands and thousands of letters and poetry, it's evident that God has always put it on my heart to be a writer. I just took a bit of a detour, but that detour shaped the words you're reading in this book. In the Bible, "full circle" moments often signify a return to a starting point, completion of a cycle, or a realization of a prophecy or plan. God is always on time, and He had a plan for me. He has a plan for you too. If you pay attention, you will notice the full-circle moments He places in your life in the days, months, and even years to come.

Journal Prompt

Dear God,

A full circle moment I've experienced during my time on this earth is _____. Please help me see when you are working to show me a full circle moment. Today, I feel like you are telling me that _____ will end up being a full-circle moment, and I can't wait to see what happens.

Day 37

Shaped by Shame

*"Those who look to him are radiant; their faces
are never covered with shame."*

Psalm 34:5

I hear from God the best when I first wake up. I receive ideas from God in my dreams, and when I wake up, I'm able to journal my thoughts to God and work to receive confirmation of what was put on my heart as I was sleeping. I am not unique in this. I have heard many people share that God woke them up in the middle of the night to speak to them. I just happen to have a lot of practice with it.

I have a friend that tells me she hears from God best at nighttime. The way I hear God may not be the way you hear from God, but the only way you can find out is through practice. That's why I gave you Journal Prompts to write to God so you can see how and when He speaks to you. I can't stress enough that you need to have your own relationship with God. This will give you the opportunity to experience what I get to experience, which is looking back and seeing if what God was putting on your heart was real, and if it actually came to fruition. My journals are such a gift. They not only help me each morning in a therapeutic way, but they reveal to me how God has been faithful all the time, and he has never forsaken me.

One of the hardest things for me to move on from was the shame I carried with me. To this day, sometimes I feel like I have a sign on my head that says "I'M BAD" when I'm invited to sit at tables where I never thought I could be. One of my biggest regrets is when Mark Cuban invited me to dinner with him and one of his colleagues to congratulate me on a job well done with my PR efforts for one of his companies. That kind of recognition was something I have always dreamed of, especially because I loved watching *Shark Tank*. I was so high on cocaine and drunk that I don't remember most of it. It was like I chose to sabotage that because I didn't feel worthy enough to be at that table.

That's what unresolved trauma and shame does. It can cause you to squander good stuff that comes your way, and you won't even recognize why you did it or how it happened so fast. I thought about how drunk I was at that dinner for nearly ten years. There had been times that people told me that I did or said horrendous things when I was drunk, and I just didn't know what I might've done that night. God was nudging me to reach out, so I did. I finally got in touch with Mark and told him I was holding onto shame and wanted to let go of it; he told me he was proud of me. The last thing I wanted to do was reach out to him, but it was one of those obedience things. I'm glad that I did because it helped me move on from feeling embarrassed.

One thing I learned from that night is it's just as triggering to have really exciting things happen as it is to have really bad things happen when you're struggling with substance use. Most of the time, I would relapse over great things happening because I wanted to celebrate. Other times it was just too much to feel so much excitement. It was like I needed to douse the fire a little bit with some alcohol. The only problem is alcohol is flammable, and so were my consequences.

The biggest consequence of all my mistakes was how I slowly became shaped by shame. It chipped away at my soul little by little, one mistake at a time. I struggled to hear what God had to say about me because I was convinced the devil was right all along: *I am never going to be that pretty girl that could be loved or valued, because I am not valuable. I am the girl that sold drugs to her dad and got arrested all the time. I am the girl that men want to have fun with, but don't want to marry.* I started to believe the lies, and I would have so much imposter syndrome and guilt when I did achieve anything great for my company.

The day I found out I was on the front cover of *D CEO Magazine* I turned off all of my lights and stayed in bed all day because I felt depressed. This was an example of me not knowing how to accept anything good. This wasn't anything I could just push away or squander. It happened; it was out there. So all I could do was hide in my house until I could process everything with God.

My walk with God has evolved now. I don't have to wait for my mornings with God to process things. I keep in communication with God all day and invite him to do life with me, not just assist me. I want to be clear. Just because I can hear from God doesn't mean I don't struggle with unworthiness or depressive thoughts. I'm just able to work through them quicker and remember who God says I am when I stay firm in the word and faithful in prayer.

I know I am very blessed to have been able to work through my shame and find freedom. Not everyone can get there, and sobriety is difficult to maintain. I watched my dad struggle with shame. He shared with me that the reason he tried meth is because someone offered it to him at work one day to help him stay awake for a project he was working on.

A lot of people in my family wondered how I was so quick to forgive my dad and why I continued to advocate for him. For starters, I loved him. But also, I understood what the shame felt like. I know what that kind of loneliness and darkness felt like. I remember that first day I tried meth, I never wanted to try it again. I bet that happened with my dad too, and many other people who end up addicted to the drug.

Looking back, I often wonder if my heart could've handled my dad choosing drugs over me. As much as I don't like what I went through, I'm glad I could understand the shame my dad carried, because it helped me take things less personal. My dad was just trying to escape his own pain and shame. He wasn't trying to harm me or hurt my feelings when he'd relapse.

When I was little, my dad tried to take his own life, just like his father did. He jumped out of the car while my mom was driving on the highway and ended up in a coma in the ICU. The family was told to make funeral arrangements. My dad had mental health struggles and unresolved trauma, and he never got the help he needed. When I was a little older my dad told me that if he died, I would be taken care of, and if he killed himself, he'd make it look like an accident, so we'd get insurance money. I was so young that I didn't really take it seriously, but now that I'm older, I know he desperately needed help and didn't know how to ask for it. If there's nothing else you get out of this book, please know that it's brave to ask for help. It does not make you weak. Asking for help is the best thing you can do for the people that love you and who need you.

During the time I got to spend with my dad before he passed away, he struggled with so much shame that he could barely face me some days. I invited him to come to one of my recovery meetings one time, and he bawled so hard that it became almost disruptive. When we left, my dad shared with me that he remembered going to his dad's recovery meetings when he was a little boy, and it was just so hard to see his daughter sitting in those same chairs. As much as I selfishly want my dad here on earth to laugh with and to do life with, I believe that God gave him grace by bringing him to heaven. God did heal him and remove his addictions just like I prayed.

Journal Prompt

Dear God,

Some ways I feel like I have been shaped by shame are
_____. Please help me remove the beliefs I am holding
onto about myself.

Day 38

What Have I Lost?

*"Instead of your shame you will receive a double portion,
and instead of disgrace you will rejoice in your inheritance.
And so you will inherit a double portion in your land,
and everlasting joy will be yours."*

Isaiah 61:7

It's time to grieve what you've lost. We cannot move on if we don't take the time to grieve. Was it your time? Your confidence? Your joy? Your freedom? Everyone has experienced loss in life. It may not have the type of loss I suffered, but it still stings, doesn't it? What have you lost that you want God to help you get back? We read in the Bible that "the Lord your God will bring you back from captivity, and have compassion on you" (Deuteronomy 30:3 nkjv). After experiencing the worst tragedies imaginable and being tested by the devil, God restored Job's losses and gave him twice of what he originally had (Job 42). This is after his friends accused him for not being a good follower of Yahweh because he had so many bad things happening to him.

About a month after my father passed away, I had to do a pitch competition that I had been working on for a year. The goal was to win the top prize of $50,000. I remember that day like it was yesterday. Right before walking on stage, I was still in my workout clothes. There was a piece of me that wanted to sabotage the entire event and walk over to the bar to get a drink. I was in a bad mood because I felt it wasn't fair that the other contestants could drink normally and calm their nerves while I had to face being nervous and grieving that my dad wasn't front row cheering me on like I had planned. I was in the green room crying and praying to God to give me strength.

At the last minute, I threw on my business jacket and attached the microphone to my collar and walked onto the stage. I started crying immediately when it became real that my dad wasn't there. I thought I had bombed it, but I didn't really care. One thing I learned about grief is it seems like nothing else matters anymore when you don't have the person you love most with you. After the other contestants gave their pitch, we were all backstage waiting to hear who won the smaller awards leading up to the big prize. One award at a time was called, and with every one, my name was called. I couldn't believe it. I also won the big prize, social innovator of the year. Confetti fell from the ceiling, and they brought out a giant check for the photo op. I remember being numb and not feeling like a winner at all because my heart was broken. I ended up winning $165,000 that night. Even though I struggled to be happy in that moment, God gave me what I needed to keep my company going when I was grieving. It seems that every time I lose something, God gives me something to help me keep going.

"My cup runs over" is a phrase that means abundance of blessings and feeling of deep gratitude. King David uses this phrase in his famous psalm (that you should memorize before the end of this book) to express thankfulness for God's provision and care.

The LORD is my shepherd;
I shall not want.
He makes me lie in green pastures;
He leads me beside still waters.
He restores my soul;
He leads me in the paths of righteousness
For his name's sake.

Yea, though I walk through the valley of the shadow of death,
I will fear no evil;
For You are with me;
Your rod and Your staff, they comfort me.

You prepare a table before me in the presence of my enemies;
You anoint my head with oil;
My cup runs over.

Surely goodness and mercy shall follow me
All the days of my life;
And I will dwell in the house of the LORD
Forever.

(Psalm 23 NKJV)

That's how I feel right now as I type these words. I feel like my cup runs over. I am so grateful for how God brought me out of darkness, and I believe he can bring you out of your version of darkness as well.

Maybe you are just now realizing some things you lost that you didn't realize you lost. That happened to me that day in the church when I felt the Holy Spirit as I listened to that song "Come Alive (Dry Bones)." I realized that I was dead, and I needed to come alive. What needs to come back alive in you?

One thing I lost is a lot of respect from people I love and care about. Over the years, my behaviors have caused others to feel pain, and I have to accept that accountability. Now that I have some sobriety under my belt and several years of therapy, I have really strong relationships and God has restored everything I lost and renewed my soul.

Journal Prompt

Dear God,

I have lost my _____. Please restore what I've lost and help me have hope in my future, as I let you comfort me while I grieve so I can be renewed and accept what you have to offer me.

Day 39

Who Have I Become?

"Search me, God, and know my heart; test me and know my anxious thoughts. See if there is any offensive way in me, and lead me in the way everlasting."

Psalm 139:23–24

In one of my keynote presentations, I often talk about the masks we wear. I was the mask wearing queen. I hid behind masks all the time to avoid vulnerability or to cover up my insecurities. The mask I wore the most was my overachieving mask. I wore burnout like it was a badge of honor. I still love to create, and I love what I do for a living, but I no longer idolize success as something that will fix my life. I know the only thing that will make me whole is Jesus Christ.

If the furthest this book goes is to just be a Christmas gift to my family, then that's enough. I don't need this book to be successful by the world's standards. I just knew I needed to write it. Do I still want to achieve success and have nice things? Of course! The best part is that I don't have the urge to squander good things when they come my way, and I can experience joy, so I'm really excited to see what God has in store for me. I am content with what he has for me now and I can lie in the green pastures and wait by the still waters while he is preparing my table for me. I am at peace. I never thought I could say that. I did not believe it was possible for me.

When I read my journals from the past, they are dark and hateful. When I read my recent journals, they are joyful and full of hope. Only God can do that. He did it for me, and I know he can do it for you. When I look back at how shame shaped me and who I became, I don't recognize that girl. When I do side-by-side comparisons, the new me is unrecognizable from the old me. God restored my soul and cleansed me from the inside out. I feel more beautiful than I've ever felt, and I feel more loved than ever. I went from believing I wasn't worthy of good things to expecting good things to happen. I went from not feeling valuable to knowing that I'm God's precious daughter, wonderfully and fearfully made. I went from thinking that I wasn't a girl that anyone would want to marry to knowing that Christ prepared me for the man of my dreams and set him aside for me. This didn't happen overnight. It took years for me of constant mornings of hearing God and walking in trust and obedience. God didn't give it all to me at once. He revealed one thing to me at a time.

For a while, I was really great at obedience, but didn't know how to trust. I struggled with surrender, I struggled with my faith, you name it, I struggled with it. God worked on my heart day in and day out. All I had to do was seek him. The Bible says it only takes mustard seed–sized faith (Matthew 17:20), and sometimes a mustard seed is all I had to give.

My biggest breakthroughs with God were when I'd come to him as I was, not trying to present myself put together. I'm talking "crying, yelling, snot dripping, fetal position, begging for mercy" type of encounters. I used to cry like that in private and deal with it by myself, then go to God and talk to Him about it. The funny thing is I thought I could compartmentalize God. Not anymore. God gets me the way I am, all the time. He created me, so He can deal with me.

What masks have you worn to protect yourself from vulnerability? What mask do you wear to cover up your insecurities? Are you able to be honest about it? It's okay if you're not. Ask God to gently reveal it to you, so you can work on it with Him. This book isn't meant to make you feel shame. It's meant to be a gentle and intimate forty days with God, so you can experience Him the way I do. As you have probably learned now that you're on Day 39, still waters really aren't boring. It's quite the adventure when you decide to do life the way God wants you to. The adjustment period of going from class V rapids to still waters isn't an easy one, but that's why I wrote this book. I want to be with you on this journey, so you don't feel like something is wrong with you when you have an urge to push away good things or have an attraction to people who hurt you. Nothing is wrong with you. You just haven't allowed Jesus to make you whole yet. You are made in his image, (Genesis 1:27), which is why the more you strive to become more like Christ, the better you begin to feel.

Journal Prompt

Dear God,

The masks I've worn are _____. These masks have caused me to become someone I'm not meant to be. Please help change the desires of my heart so they can be aligned with your will. I know the life you have for me is far better than what I could imagine.

Day 40

Who Do I Want to Be?

"For we live by faith, not by sight."

2 Corinthians 5:7

Day 40. You did it. I wish I was sitting there next to you hearing how God has worked in your life and how He has revealed Himself to you. I know he has. If He hasn't, He will. Continue to seek Him and ask for guidance.

The last assignment is to re-do the first assignment. Remember before you started this forty-day journey, I had you write down a list of affirmations for where you want to be in the next five years? Take a look at that list. Has anything changed? Were some of those desires deriving from fear, pride, masks you wear, or insecurities? Look back at who you wanted to be and ask God to help you rewrite it for who He wants you to be.

I'm embarrassed to admit that before I was able to hear God like I do now, my list had success and money as a priority, with God and family at the bottom. Now, I have changed so much that I can completely flip that piece of paper upside down. In fact, I did turn it upside down and tape it on my bathroom mirror as a reminder of what comes first in my life and where God brought me from. Now, God and family are number one on my list of priorities and success and money are at the bottom. What I can do on my own or what I can achieve is no longer my identity. My identity is in Christ, and I can do all things through him who gives me strength. (Philippians 4:13).

Journal Prompt

Dear God,

Thank you for _____

_____.

Epilogue

December 25, 2025

Dear God,

I'm coming up on seven years sober. On Christmas Day of 2018, You rescued me from alcohol. Giving myself the gift of sobriety hasn't been easy, but it's been worth it. I've been able to hear You so much better sober. It's like my Wi-Fi signal to heaven is stronger. ☺ The greatest gift I have, though, is my relationship with You. It's a gift that keeps on giving day in and day out. Your promise in Your Word that You will restore everything I've lost. Over the past twenty years, I've lost so much, but I've gained much more.

I'm Mrs. Norris now! I got married on November 22, 2025, and two of my bridesmaids I met in that Christian business forum. I wrote those "Dear future husband" letters for several years, and I gave Ben the entire book of letters as a wedding gift. I was afraid to give my heart to another man, but I realized it's You that holds my heart. My mentor was right. You revealed to me when the time was right to know Ben was the one you chose for me. It's a new beginning, like when Simon became Peter.

Three months before my wedding, I came across a journal entry I had written five years ago. It was about a dream You had given me about who my husband would be. It described Ben to a T. I couldn't believe it. What shocked me more, is the journal entry was written on Nov 22. The same date as my wedding that I had been planning with complete trepidation! How divine that You gave me that dream before I even met Ben, and had me journal about it on the exact date of the wedding I never knew I would have.

But You knew. You have always known, and you have always provided.

I prayed and prayed wondering why You made me walk in fear with a blindfold on, but now I get it. You were teaching me to trust You, and for that, I am so grateful.

We decided to go to Disney World for our honeymoon, because I did in fact get my happily ever after that I prayed for in that Budget Suites motel twenty years ago.

Growing up, I thought the Disney princesses had their curses broken by receiving love from a man. But that wasn't the process, it was the result. They attracted the love they projected. The princesses had to first believe there was something better for them and love themselves enough to go after it. They had to keep faith that everything would work out even when every-thing was going wrong. Fear did not stop them from believing, and that's how curses are broken.

I faced my fears and went after what I know You had for me and believed it would be good even when things were hard. Your grace is what I always needed. The irony is, I always had it. I just needed to believe it.

Today is my dad's birthday. I miss him so much. He would've been sixty-two. I flipped to psalm 62, curious for what you had for me. It is about trusting in You completely, especially during hard times. That sums up this book pretty well. Thank you for always giving me confirmation. Let my dad know that for his birthday we broke a generational curse. Oh, and ask him if he's ready to be a grandpa because I'm no longer afraid to move forward with starting a family. ☺

As tempting as it is to forget the past and move forward, I can't deny what the past has taught me about You and myself after reading through all those journals. I don't just love the new me. I love all of me, even the bad, because it was through the bad that I found You. As You have taught us in Your Word, I rejoice in my trials now because I know You are shaping me to be in alignment with Your will for Your purpose—a purpose far greater than I could even imagine or ask for. Although I feel as if a curse was broken in my own fairytale, I know it's a daily surrender. But I no longer surrender in suffering, I surrender in peace and joy.

The best is yet to come.

Love, Cheri Norris

Your Next 40 Days

This is a guide to get started with daily reading of the Bible and journaling over the next forty days, so you can continue to practice hearing God while using his Word.

Day 1–31: Read a chapter of Proverbs each day
Day 32: Read Ephesians 6:11–17
Day 33: Read 1 Peter 5:8–11
Day 34: Read Romans 12:2–3
Day 35: Read Matthew 6:24–34
Day 36: Read James 1:12–27
Day 37: Read Luke 15:4–7
Day 38: Read Colossians 2:2–10
Day 39: Read 2 Timothy 1:7–9
Day 40: Read Galatians 5:13–26

www.ingramcontent.com/pod-product-compliance
Lightning Source LLC
Chambersburg PA
CBHW020249130626
46549CB00005B/2144